# Performing Mourning
## Laments in Contemporary Art

Guy Cools

Antennae-Arts in Society
Valiz, Amsterdam

# Performing Mourning
*Laments in Contemporary Art*

Guy Cools

For my parents,
François Cools (1941–1970) and Charlotte Reyns

And my sons Filip, Steven and Julian

# Contents

# Introduction:
A Personal Story

From October 26, 1977, the day after his mother died, until
September 15, 1979, only a few months before his own death,
Roland Barthes kept a diary of his mourning on 330 'fact sheets'
that he had cut from ordinary sheets of paper. This diary was posthumously published in 2009. Referencing Proust, Barthes prefers
to talk of his grief (*chagrin*) instead of his mourning (*deuil*), which
he describes as a permanent state that will never leave him nor
diminish over time. His only choice is to attempt to transform the
state of his grief 'from a static state into a fluid one.'[2]

Most psychological literature makes a distinction between
grief and mourning. Grief is the interiorized state. It is 'the expression of the loss of relationship, and the most common experience
we all must face, over and over again.'[3] Mourning is the necessary
process of exteriorization. Grief is private, while mourning is public. In her 2017 book *Grief Works*, the psychotherapist Julia Samuel
writes that grief is 'the emotional reaction to a loss, in this case to
death,' whereas mourning is 'the process we have to go through to
adjust to the world in which the person has died.'[4] Grief includes a
range of different emotions that we experience and express in our
mourning, with sadness and anger being the principal ones. Grief's
sadness always involves a loss of energy. At the extreme end of the
spectrum, its pathology is depression. Grief's anger temporarily
increases energy levels. At the extreme end of the spectrum, its
pathology is mania. Freud differentiated between mourning and
melancholia, considering mourning a healthy working out of feelings of grief and melancholia a pathology in which the mourner
remains stuck in his or her attachment to absence or loss.

In their popular but also highly criticized work *On Grief and
Grieving: Finding the Meaning of Grief Through the Five Stages
of Loss* (2005), Elisabeth Kübler-Ross and her co-author David
Kessler apply the five stages that she first identified as being
part of the process of dying (i.e., suffering through a terminal
illness) to the process of grieving for any kind of personal loss.
The five stages are:

> Denial: shock and disbelief that the loss has occurred
> Anger: that someone we love is no longer there
> Bargaining: all the what-ifs and regrets
> Depression: sadness from the loss
> Acceptance: acknowledging the reality of the loss.[5]

In his more recent sequel, Kessler adds a sixth stage: *Finding Meaning* (2019). As Barthes repeatedly points out, we do not pass through these stages in a linear way. They are discontinuous and we often have to revisit them, spiraling through many iterations. The American poet Linda Pastan wrote a poem with the title *The Five Stages of Grief*. Each section of the poem deals with one of the five stages, but the last lines question this too neat journey: 'But something is wrong. Grief is a circular staircase. I have lost you.'[6]

In another classic work on grief, *A Grief Observed* (1961, 2015), C.S. Lewis documents his thoughts as he mourns for his wife Joy Davidman. He opens with the lines: 'No one ever told me that grief felt so like fear. I am not afraid, but the sensation is like being afraid. The same fluttering in the stomach, the same restlessness, the yawning.'[7] And he continues:

> For in grief nothing 'stays put.' One keeps on emerging from a phase, but it always recurs. Round and round. Everything repeats. Am I going in circles, or dare I hope I am on a spiral? But if a spiral, am I going up or down it?[8]

The author Hilary Mantel, when asked to comment on Lewis's book, said: 'The work of mourning, if not performed when it is due, seems to be stored up for us, often for many years.'[9]

It is not always easy to draw a distinction between grief and mourning. The line dividing one from the other is easily blurred, as more poetic voices in literature acknowledge. Julian Barnes, for example, writes in *Levels of Life* (2013):

> There is the question of grief versus mourning. You can try to differentiate them by saying that grief is a state while mourning is a process; yet they inevitably overlap. Is the state diminishing? Is the process progressing? How to tell? It's easier to think of them metaphorically. Grief is vertical—and vertiginous—while mourning is horizontal.

> Grief makes your stomach turn, snatches the breath from you, cuts off the blood supply to the brain; mourning blows you in a new direction.[10]

The topic of this book is mourning. It is something that I have carried with me for most of my life, as the second part of this introduction will explain. For the last twenty years, I have been researching the topic in a more conscious manner. The result is this publication, together with a number of artistic projects that have been created alongside it. In *Levels of Life*, Julian Barnes also states that grief, like death, is both 'banal and unique.' He makes a

> banal comparison. When you change your make of car, you suddenly notice how many other cars of the same sort there are on the road. They register in a way they never did before. When you are widowed, you suddenly notice all the widows and widowers coming towards you.[11]

Similarly, when I resolved to work on this book, I was struck by the overwhelming number of contemporary art practices I was encountering that were dealing with mourning. The subject is vast and for each of the works discussed in this book there are many others that are equally relevant and interesting. Since I don't intend to give an encyclopedic overview, I had to find some kind of criterium—to limit myself. As in my previous books, *In-Between Dance Cultures: On the Migratory Artistic Identity of Sidi Larbi Cherkaoui and Akram Khan* (2015) and *Imaginative Bodies: Dialogues in Performance Practices* (2016), I am mainly interested in writing about creative processes: how artists think, work and imagine. This is what I do as a (dance) dramaturg—I accompany these processes. With a few exceptions of iconic examples that I could not ignore or that touched me personally, I have focused mainly on works that I have collaborated on and on artists with whom I have at least had some direct contact. This meant that I was able to exchange ideas with them, ask questions, and include their own voices in my writing. My focus, as usual, is on dance and on how the body somatically 'performs mourning.' However, since this topic is omnipresent in all artistic disciplines, the examples will cover a much broader range of art forms and inter-disciplinary practices, including literature, performing arts, music, and visual arts.

Shortly before this manuscript was ready to be sent to the publisher, the research center The Culture of Grief at Aarhus University organized an online conference entitled *The Culture of Grief: Philosophy, Ecology and Politics of Loss in the Twenty-first Century*.[12] The conference consisted of four in-depth interviews with the philosophers and cultural theorists Judith Butler, Simon Critchley, Jonathan Lear, and Arne Johan Vetlesen, who talked about how 'grief can be thought as an existential and political concept and how it might guide and even transform our thinking of the current global and ecological situation.' The American philosopher and psychoanalyst Jonathan Lear argued convincingly that mourning is a 'constitutive activity of being human' and that in order to grow we need to develop 'the ability to bid adieu to earlier ways of living and being.' Judith Butler, meanwhile, called for us 'to turn our grief into mobilization. Grieve and act.' The conference reiterated many of the themes of this book and included some of the voices I had already woven into my text. It also made me realize that, as with most academic discourses, philosophical and psychoanalytic discussions of grief are mired in hierarchical thinking. Critchley, for example, dismissed Elisabeth Kübler-Ross's work as 'crypto-Buddhism.' Artists, by contrast, generally don't discriminate against their sources in such a way. They use whatever inspires them, including the above-mentioned 'highbrow' academic discourses, but equally more 'lowbrow' genres such as psychoanalytic self-help books (often containing concrete case studies), fiction, and popular myths and beliefs from their own cultures. In a similar way, I have tried not to discriminate between different discourses and genres, referencing and interweaving many of them into my own narrative, wherever relevant.

As a result, I quote from an eclectic range of literary genres, drawing on everything from academic texts to (auto)biographical writing and poetry. This eclecticism mirrors the abundance of sources that many artists seek out for inspiration and then translate and integrate into their work. It also reflects the diversity of languages that they use to create a discourse around their work. In writing this book, I have frequently made use of research and insights from the fields of both anthropology and psychology. However, I am neither an anthropologist nor a psychologist. My perspective is that of a dramaturg who accompanies contemporary art processes.

Experiencing firsthand her daughter's Rachel mourning process after her future son-in-law died unexpectedly in an accident, the Canadian journalist Katherine Ashenburg wrote *The Mourner's Dance: What We Do When People Die* (2002). Ashenburg's book is a well-researched and documented account of funeral and mourning rituals in the main communities she is connected to, including: the (Irish-)Catholic, the Greek and the Jewish communities. She also makes some interesting observations on the existing literature on the topic. In 2001, when she was writing her book, she counted more than 2500 titles on grief, available on Amazon, a lot of them self-help books. She confirms the thesis that I will develop in the following chapter that in order to deal with their mourning, people often feel the need to write about it. She also advocates a similar, non-hierarchical approach to this large body of existing literature, offering its readers consolation.

> Even well-intentioned family and friends may become impatient or bored or frustrated with the trajectory of grief. Self-help authors do not. Nor do the authors of memoirs, such as C.S. Lewis. ... Mourning is an extreme of loneliness, and these disparate books keep the mourner company, even if only briefly, on her long, solitary path.[13]

One purpose of this book is to look at laments, both in their original form and in contemporary art practices, as ways of *performing mourning* in front of an audience of witnesses. Performances of this kind allow emotions of grief to be fully experienced and expressed, helping those who are grieving to avoid becoming stuck in static grief. 'Each person's grief is as unique as their fingerprint. But what everyone has in common is that no matter how they grieve, they share a need for their grief to be witnessed.'[14] Like grief itself, the performance of mourning is unique to every person. Sometimes it takes a whole lifetime or an entire artistic oeuvre to complete it. Performing your mourning does not diminish or resolve your grief, but it allows you to fully live it.

The writing of this book was never a linear process. It has been spread out over many years and was interrupted several times. As a freelance dramaturg and artist, I am continually fighting to make time for writing and to find a sustainable way of combining it with other professional engagements and with my family role as a husband and father. I was able to write a first outline of this book during my second residence at the International Research Center 'Interweaving Performance Cultures' at the Freie Universität in Berlin, in 2016. The support I received from the team at the Institute and from my colleagues motivated me to continue and deepen my research. Since then, I have made several attempts to create the material conditions to do so. In 2017, I was offered a post-doctoral fellowship by the Onassis Foundation to spend six months in Athens to work on this book, which I had to turn down because my son Julian had just been born and the new family situation did not allow for a long period away from home. I also felt much too happy during this time to give all my attention to the topic of mourning, although the experience of having a new baby did inspire me to add the final chapter on lullabies. In the end, it feels like a meaningful synchronicity that it is the Covid-19 crisis that offered me an unexpected sabbatical from my other engagements so I could finish this manuscript.

We can only tell the stories that we own. But in our complex present-day reality, all of our stories have become hybrids that are often composed of fragments of other stories from all the people and cultures we have been in contact with, including the stories of our ancestors. Let me conclude this introduction by telling you my personal story.

On July 30, 1970, my father François Cools died in a car accident, a fortnight before his twenty-ninth birthday and less than three weeks after my sixth. In accordance with the spirit of the time, or perhaps also because of the violence of his unexpected death, it was judged that it would be 'unhealthy' for me to attend his funeral. I was not allowed to perform my mourning. As a result, I interiorized my grief and got stuck in it. In the Greek tradition of the *moirológhia* one uses the expression 'he went un-cried,' which is indicative of a 'bad death.'[15] Both Kessler and Samuel explicitly describe how important it is for children to be allowed to be part of the funeral rites.

> We think we can spare our children pain by not exposing them to the reality of death. But the opposite is true. ... Going to a funeral will help because they, too, need to have their pain witnessed, to feel it reflected in the emotions of those around them.[16]

Samuel adds that children experience this 'protection as an exclusion,' which may eventually lead to 'resentment towards their surviving parent.'[17] In his book *The New Black: Mourning, Melancholia and Depression* (2008), the British psychoanalyst Darian Leader also explores what can happen when a loss in the family has not been openly mourned. 'What consequences will this have, we can ask, on the children? How can they mourn if they are deprived of the very possibility of a dialogue of mournings?'[18] Leader thus emphasizes the importance of the mourning process being acknowledged, seen, and shared. 'As humans don't we need others to authenticate our losses? To recognize them as losses rather than to pass over them in silence? Don't we need, in other word, a dialogue of mournings?'[19] Seeing other people mourn allows us to better access our own mourning.

Similarly to how Barthes describes it in his diary, my own grief continued to exist in a 'discontinuous' way. Its anger and sadness could pop up at any moment, triggered by the most trivial incidents such as spilling a cup of water or watching a television series. My birthday in particular became a very volatile moment that often ended with me crying and shouting that there was no reason to celebrate or receive gifts. Another incident that left a strong impression on me was my great-grandfather's funeral. I was eleven years old when he died. The funeral was held in his native village where it was still customary to follow the coffin from the church to the graveyard. My father had been my great-grandfather's eldest grandson and tradition had it that he should walk at the front of the procession, but since he, too, was dead, I as his oldest son had to replace him. Walking behind my great-grandfather's coffin, I felt both a huge responsibility and a burning anger at the injustice of the order of events. Throughout my childhood my outbursts were tolerated and ascribed to my oversensitive nature, but as I got older, they no longer seemed socially appropriate. I began to interiorize them more and more.

My mother's way of dealing with her emotions was to never show them. She also never talked about my father—although a black-and-white photograph of him occupied a central place of honor in our living room. My mother never remarried or had any other close male friends. I didn't dare ask her the questions I had about my father's death, as I was afraid to upset her. Instead, my imagination filled in the gaps. For instance, for a very long time I cherished the memory of waking up in the night that my father had died; I remembered going into my parents' bedroom and finding my grandmother in bed next to my mother instead of him. Much later I found out that on the night of the accident I had been on holiday in the countryside with my grandparents. Maybe the event did happen at a later time and I just displaced it in time. Memory and imagination became intertwined and veiled by my suppressed emotions.

My interiorized grief, especially the anger associated with it, also fundamentally destabilized the balance of energy in my body. For one thing, I had an overdose of energy and did not require much rest, being a restless sleeper who often woke from terrible nightmares. The fuel for this abundance of energy may have been a negative one, but it drove my professional career forward at high speed. By my mid-twenties I had already accumulated a lot of responsibilities. The speed at which I moved forward meant that I ran the risk of missing some turns in the road. In my late twenties, this suspended state of interiorized grief led to serious physical and mental health problems, which were directly triggered by increasingly frequent periods of insomnia.

As Robert Pogue Harrison states in *The Dominion of the Dead* (2003), the codified, socially understood language of the lament is a way for an individual to perform the process of mourning and thus allow the work of separation to take place. If it fails, the consequences can be serious:

> instead of the dead dying in me, I die with the dead—either through excessive identification with the corpse ... or through an inability to articulate my grief, which leads to any number of discrete, yet no less dangerous, pathologies.[20]

After one too many personal crises, I entered traditional psychotherapy to begin to deal with these issues, slowly becoming more conscious of them. I also started to gently press my mother for information, asking some of the questions that had gone unanswered for so long. I was curious about the exceptional bond she seemed to have with my dead father, who came from a social background that was different from hers. These were first steps in exteriorizing my grief. However, rationalizing and objectifying are not enough. Eventually, the unexpressed emotions need to be relived somatically.

In the summer of 1999, at the age of 35, almost exactly on the same day that my father had died 29 years before, I had an extremely emotional breakdown that was triggered by the ending of a new romantic relationship. I cried for hours and felt completely paralyzed by a deep state of depression that affected both my mind and my body. I was only able to overcome this state when I realized that I was not only crying for the present but also for my unlived past. After this realization, I felt completely empty—the energy of anger that had been my driver for many years had completely gone. It took the rest of the summer holidays for me to recover. Shortly afterwards I began practicing yoga, replacing the negative energy source with a more positive one. I was also able to share some of my mourning with my mother and at the moment of doing this, I felt a strong energetic shift happening in our relationship. A couple of years later this cycle repeated itself when we both stood at the bed of my dying grandfather (my mother's father) and were able to share our mourning during his funeral rites.

Exactly one year after I re-lived my original mourning process, I visited Greece to participate in the first Summer Academy of the National Theatre of Greece, on the invitation of Eleni Varopoulou. It was there that I discovered the living tradition of the *moirológhia*—but that is another story, which I will tell in chapter three.

In *Precarious Life: The Powers of Mourning and Violence* (2004), Judith Butler formulates the hypothesis that the process of mourning implies acceptance:

> By the loss one undergoes one will be changed, possibly forever. Perhaps mourning has to do with agreeing to undergo a transformation (perhaps one should say *submitting* to a transformation) the full result of which one cannot know in advance.[21]

The different stages of my own mourning—the failure to express it, the pathology of repeating it in an uncontrolled and discontinuous way, rationalizing and then re-living it—have all been moments of transformation, of giving over to a not-knowing.

This book is the chronicle of a lifelong journey that has become more conscious and focused over the past two decades. As such, many of the topics that are being dealt with here could easily be developed further into several separate studies. I invite the reader to read it as travel guide, that is, an introduction to different sites and landmarks that deserve to be explored and experienced in a deeper way when you visit them yourself.

# Notes

1    Barthes 2009, p. 167. 'Au deuil intériorisé, il n'y a guère de signes. C'est l'accomplissement de l'intériorité absolue. Toutes les sociétés sages, cependant, ont prescrit et codifié l'extériorisation du deuil. Malaise de la notre en ce qu'elle nie le deuil.' Except otherwise mentioned, all translations are my own

2    Ibid., p. 154.

3    Savage 2018, p. xi.

4    Samuel 2017, p. xvii.

5    In: Kessler 2019, p. 1. The Kübler-Ross model has only descriptive value in the way it describes the different experiences people have, always in a non-linear and incomplete way. The criticism is valid if the model is applied prescriptive or linear.

6    Pastan, quoted in Kanter 2007, pp. 43–44.

7    Lewis 1961, 2015, p. 3.

8    Ibid., pp. 45–46.

9    Mantel in C.S. Lewis 1961, 2015, p. 65.

10    Barnes 2013, p. 88.

11    Ibid., p. 70.

12    For the integral recording of the conference, see: youtu.be/0JBPQik2-x8.

13    Ashenburg 2003, p. 156.

14    Kessler 2019, p. 29.

15    See for instance Varvantakis 2013, p. 20.

16    Kessler 2019, p. 45.

17    Samuel 2017, pp. 92–93.

18    Leader 2008, p. 80.

19    Ibid., p. 85.

20    Harrison 2003, p. 58.

21    Butler 2004, p. 21.

# Elegiac Literature: Mourning as a Motivation to Write

> For if poetry has the power to make the naught resound,
> if it has the power to house, bury and commune with the
> dead, it is because its rhythms, accents, and elegiac tones
> have their elemental source in human grief.[1]

In the introduction to *The New Black, Mourning, Melancholia and Depression*, Darian Leader mentions that the lack of clinical, scientific literature on the subject is compensated by the fact that 'all literature' deals with mourning. It leads him to reflect on the question, 'what place did the arts have in the process of mourning?'[2] Throughout his discussion of the clinical aspects of the mourning process, he continues to give examples of artists who have explicitly dealt with mourning and often built an entire oeuvre on it. One such example is Edgar Allan Poe, whose mother died a month before his third birthday. According to some accounts, he was left alone with her corpse and a babysitter overnight. His oeuvre is full of corpses, premature burials, ghosts, and people coming back from the dead. 'Poe's literary effort to describe this encounter with death from every possible angle suggests that the work of mourning could not be completed.'[3]

Leader repeats his question about the relationship between the arts and mourning several times. 'What place, after all, do literature, theater, cinema and the other visual and plastic arts have in human cultures? Could their very existence be linked to the human necessity to mourn?'[4] One of his conclusions is that the arts not only facilitate the expression of grief, but also provide something that goes beyond it: the creative act shows that there is a life still to be lived. 'The arts exist to allow us to access grief, and they do this by showing publicly how creation can emerge from the turbulence of a human life.'[5]

The French writer Philippe Forest created an entire literary oeuvre around his grief for his daughter who died at the age of four: his works include, among others, *L'Enfant éternel* (*The Eternal Child*, 1997); *Sarinagara* (2004), *Tous les enfants sauf un* (All children except one, 2007). In a series of dialogues with the philosopher Vincent Delecroix, he talks about his grief as a burning source of creativity. He also defends his right to remain in a state of inconsolable grief. The title of the dialogues, *Le deuil: Entre le chagrin et le néant* (2015), is a quote by William Faulkner: 'Between grief and nothing, I will take grief.'

In their dialogues, Forest and Delecroix discuss how much of our literary heritage is in fact elegiac: from Homer to Sophocles (particularly his *Antigone*), and from Shakespeare to Dostoevsky, Proust, and Joyce. 'In the end all literature creates *personas*, effigies, characters—to draw the portrait of those who are absent. It is an art of mourning.'[6] They also reject the belief that a simple, analytic naming of the traumatic experience of loss has a therapeutic value in itself. Forest even denies the need for healing or recovery. He says that the only thing that can be done is to bear witness to one's own (or another's) grief. By sharing it, one can create a collectivity around what is in essence a lonely experience. In his novel *Sarinagara*, he links his individual grief to the collective grief that arose when the atomic bomb fell on Nagasaki, embracing his own feelings of 'survivor's guilt.' The last sentence of the novel reads: 'unforgivable, even if innocent, we that are alive.'[7] He also rejects the notion that the purpose of Greek tragedy should be a cathartic reintegration into society: 'literature, since antiquity ... doesn't console one's grief but protests against it.'[8]

Referring to a work by Nicole Loraux, *Les Mères en deuil* (*Mothers in Mourning*, 1989), Forest acknowledges that in classical literature, mourning is a predominantly feminine and maternal activity. Mourning thus puts a man in touch with his feminine side. Delecroix in turn refers to Hegel's discussion of the 'marvelous institution of the lamenters' as an example of how 'rituals mime and stage pain' and how 'they socially objectify the intimate, subjective pain.'[9]

The list of elegiac literature is endless. In high school I remember only appreciating my own, Dutch, literary heritage by reading *Uitvaert van mijn dochterken* (Funeral of my daughter, 1633) by the seventeenth-century poet and playwright Joost van de Vondel. At university my admiration for Seamus Heaney was very much based on the last verse of his poem *Mid-Term Break*, in which he describes coming home after his younger brother was killed in a car accident:

> Wearing a poppy bruise on his left temple,
> He lay in the four foot box as in his cot.
> No gaudy scars, the bumper knocked him clear.
>
> A four foot box, a foot for every year.[10]

Some of the most successful contemporary literature is elegiac in nature. Yann Martel's award-winning novel *Life of Pi* (2001) is

well known for the surreal story it tells of a survivor who fictional-izes his survival. But Martel's entire oeuvre deals with mourning. His debut story, *The Facts behind the Helsinki Roccamatios* (1993), chronicles his coming to terms with a friend's death from AIDS. *Beatrice and Virgil* (2010) is an allegoric tale about representations of the Holocaust, and *The High Mountains of Portugal* (2016) is a story in which all the main characters are in a liminal state of grief which sets them apart from the rest of society. They start walking backwards, choose a chimpanzee as a surrogate partner, or retreat as far away as possible from urban society to the high mountains of Portugal.

    *Self* (1996) presents itself as a semi-autobiographical novel in which the narrator, who is characterized by a lover as 'the saddest guy I ever met,'[11] comes of age and finds his own voice as an author. His journey through childhood, adolescence, and adulthood is interspersed with smaller and bigger moments of 'unacknowledged loss,' such as finding a dead sea turtle on the beach as a child and suffering through the end of a friendship or a love relationship. However, there are also two more serious, in-depth, transformative experiences of grief. The first one is when both his parents die in a plane crash when he is still an adolescent. 'I relegated my grief to the dark basement of my consciousness, there to swim about and have the effects that Freudians will delight in surmising.'[12] The long-term impact of this grief on the author is such that he literally transforms —crossing over physically to the other gender. She continues to grow into adulthood with the guilt of living on 'the blood money' of her parents' inheritance. But her female self will transform again after another traumatic experience: she is raped and the resulting pregnancy ends in a miscarriage.

> I don't know why they call it rape. To me it was murder. I was killed that day and I've had to drag death around in me ever since, a roaming greyness in my colorful interior; sometimes it's my stomach that's dead, sometimes my head, sometimes my intestines, often my heart.[13]

The experience of grief is first and foremost a somatic experience and writing is a way to fill the void. 'This is as close as I can come to an explanation of why I started to write: not for the sake of writing, but for the sake of company.'[14]

After the death of his life partner Pat Kavanagh in 2008, Julian Barnes wrote several works which are not only dedicated to her, but which are also elegiac in nature. The most explicit elegy is the third part of his book *Levels of Life* (2013), entitled 'The Loss of Depth.' It is a diary of his grief, not unlike Roland Barthes's diary of mourning. He writes:

> Early in life, the world divides crudely into those who have had sex and those who haven't. Later, into those who have known love, and those who haven't. Later still—at least, if we are lucky (or, on the other hand, unlucky)—it divides into those who have endured grief, and those who haven't. These divisions are absolute; they are tropics we cross.[15]

In Max Porter's book *Grief is the Thing with Feathers* (2015), the process of mourning by a father for his dead wife and his two sons for their dead mother is accompanied by an imaginary crow. Small, discontinuous anecdotes and stories are told from the different perspectives of the DAD, the BOYS, and CROW. Sometimes the different voices enter into dialogue with each other:

> Man: I would be done grieving?
> Bird: No, not at all. You were done being hopeless. Grieving is something you're still doing, and something you don't need a crow for.
> Man: I agree. It changes all the time.[16]

Full of black humor, the short novel shows how each individual, even in a tight family unit, experiences grief in a completely unique way. For those not affected by it, it is impossible to understand these solitary, interiorized processes.

> I was becoming expert in the behaviour of orbiting grievers. Being at the epicentre grants a curiously anthropological awareness of everybody else; the overwhelmeds, the affect-edly lackadaisicals, the nothing so fars, the overstayers, the new best friends of hers, of mine, of the boys.[17]

For the protagonist of Porter's book, as for so many others, grief eventually leads to an obsession with writing. The boys chart the transformations that their dad undergoes: 'He was young and good

and sometimes funny. He was silent then he was livid then he was spiteful and unfamiliar, then he became obsessed and had visions and wrote and wrote and wrote.'[18]

In her autobiographical story 'Project for a Trip to China', Susan Sontag interweaves descriptions of her preparations for a visit to communist China with accounts of childhood memories and quotes by writers such as Mao Zedong and Freud. The story is nothing but a series of short, aphoristic paragraphs. Slowly the reader begins to realize that there is a connection between Sontag's present desire to visit China and the lifelong absence of her father, who died from tuberculosis while he was working in China as a fur trader in 1939. Sontag was only five years old at the time. 'Whose voice is the voice of the person who wants to go to China? A child's voice. Less than six years old.'[19]

All stories are unique, but we are particularly touched by stories that resemble our own. This lies at the heart of mimesis and empathy. Sontag's story moved me more than many others I had read. She in turn mentions that she still weeps 'in any movie with a scene in which a father returns home after a long desperate absence, at the moment when he hugs his child.'[20] Her trip to China is part of Sontag's ongoing process of mourning. 'He died so far away. By visiting my father's death, I make him heavier. I will bury him myself.'[21] His absence also marks her relationship with her mother M., whom she addresses in a letter never sent. 'Dearest M. I cannot telephone. I am six years old. My grief falls like snowflakes on the warm soil of your indifference. You are inhaling your own pain.'[22] Sontag's own son David is placed in an intergenerational triangulation with his dead grandfather. 'David wears my father's ring.'[23] 'Death doesn't die,'[24] but we can forgive the dead as well as the living for abandoning us. 'I shall forgive my father. For dying.— Shall David forgive his? (Not for dying.) For him to decide.'[25] The death of a family member affects everyone else in the family, even those who are not yet born. It changes the entire constellation of relational dynamics. It is probably not too far-fetched to conclude that Sontag's prolific output as a writer was a way for her to fill the void of her father's absence.

Katie Kitamura's novel *A Separation* (2017) tells the story of a woman who travels to Greece to ask her unfaithful husband for a divorce, only to find that he has been murdered. It is part psychological romance, focusing on the triangulation between the narrator, her husband, and her mother-in-law, and part murder mystery or whodunit. The process of grieving it describes is complex, as the pain of loss becomes intertwined with other wounds, in this case the infidelity of the husband. In addition, the narrator feels guilt for not having told her mother-in-law about the separation. There is also the violence of the murder, which remains unsolved.

> They say that there are five stages of grief, that things get worse before they get better, and in the end time does indeed heal all wounds. But what about the wounds you do not know you do not know about, and the course of which you cannot predict?[26]

What makes *A Separation* even more pertinent for my own research is that the novel is set in Mani, and that the dead husband, Christopher, went there to write a study on the local tradition of the *moirológhia*. 'Christopher had almost certainly come to Greece in order to study its professional mourners, the women who were paid to issue lamentations at funerals. ... What intrigued him about the practice was its externalization of grief.'[27] The narrator visits one of the *moirológhistas*, who shares with her meaningful insights into her craft (which I will discuss in detail in the next chapter). 'And I learned, they taught me first to sing, then to channel the sadness that is necessary to weeping. ... You need to have a great deal of sadness inside you to mourn for other people.'[28]

As you may have derived from the above paragraphs, I am an avid and eclectic reader. From a very young age I would go to the local library several times a week and devour five volumes—the allowed maximum—within the next 48 hours. My reading and my mourning were my two main motivations to start writing myself. A lot of my earliest writing was a dialogue with my absent father.

In the practice of *Rewriting Distance*,[29] an improvised performance practice that I developed with the Canadian choreographer Lin Snelling, there are some stories that appear over and over again. One of these is the story of Jerome, my childhood tortoise. Every summer, Jerome was a favorite playmate in the little suburban garden behind our house. And every autumn before the first frost, Jerome had to be brought inside and put in a box full of straw in the cellar so that he could hibernate. One autumn, however, we were too late. Jerome had already dug himself into the earth and disappeared—for forever, as it turned out. When he resurfaced in the spring, it must have been on the other side of the wall, in one of our neighbors' gardens. I never saw him again. Having told the story many times, I no longer know how much of it is true and how much of it I have fictionalized in my memory. But the fact that it is a story about a childhood trauma of loss seems to be very relevant, given the much larger trauma I lived through as a child.

When I read Hélène Cixous's autobiographical texts on writing, *Writing Blind: Conversation with a Donkey* in *Stigmata* (1998) and *'Coming to Writing' and Other Essays* (1991), I was struck by the similarities and differences to my own journey. I was born in an Antwerp suburb in 1964 to a fairly homogenous white, middle-class family (with only some minor social differences between my mother's ancestors, who were craftspeople, and the miners and cobblers on my father's side). I never had to deal with the issues of foreignness and exclusion that Cixous battled with. But as it did for her, my voracious reading came out of a need to fill an emptiness, a lack, and an absence. My early writings were 'a way of not being able to go through with mourning for death.'[30]

In the end, all of writing and all stories are about the body. In Cixous's words:

> I don't 'begin' by 'writing': I don't write. Life becomes text starting out from the body. I am already text. History, love, violence, time, work, desire inscribe it in my body, I go where the 'fundamental language' is spoken, the body language.[31]

The same thesis is explored by Stanley Keleman and Joseph Campbell in a series of dialogues that were published by Keleman under the title *Myth & the Body* (1999). In it they discuss how all myths, all stories told, are about the body—its birth, its death and all the stages of transformation in between. Mythology is to society and language what DNA is to science, that is, the accumulated history of our individual and common genealogy: 'A mythic image is the shape of anatomy speaking about itself.' The 'serpent,' for instant, represents the spinal cord and the 'crown of thorns' or the 'thousand-petaled lotus' are images for the cortex.[32] We create these 'evocative images' and tell our stories 'to touch and resonate the very deep centers of our impulse system, and to move us into action.'[33] The images and stories enable us to trans-form, even on the level of body metabolism.

My best writing moments (and also the moments when the *Rewriting Distance* practice becomes most alive for its participants and those in the audience) are when the images and stories that have been created resonate on a deep, somatic level. The story of Jerome is such a story. It only resurfaces when it is needed, that is when someone who is listening for it summons it.

> Through a philosophy of listening whereby the most archaic images rise to a symbolic level in order to speak, we may gain some familiarity with the personal and group archetypes that, in the most imaginary ways, talk of fall, exile and loss, just as they do of restoration, mutation and awareness. In my opinion something can 'speak' if it is listened to.[34]

Some of the literary works mentioned above are based on autobiographical facts, while others are crafted works of fiction, but I believe that there is always another story of mourning hiding beneath the fiction. Mourning a pet tortoise, for example, can be a fiction that masks another, more real grief. The important thing is the need to tell the stories, to share them with others, and by doing so to make the underlying grief communal.

In my creative practice and also in my life I have frequently experienced the principle of synchronicity. Even now, as I am reflecting on Jerome, my Viennese friend Isolde Fitzel sends me a poem by the German poet Christian Morgenstern, entitled *Die Schildkröte* (tortoise). It ends with the following lines:

> *Ich kenne nicht des Todes Bild*
> *und nicht des Sterbens Nöte:*
> *Ich bin die Schild–ich bin die Schild–*
> *ich bin die Schild–krö–kröte.*

In my own personal, creative translation this would read:

> I haven't been beyond death's hurdle
> Nor do I know the notes 'der Tod'
> I am the turtle–I am the turtle–
> I am the turtle–to–toad

The tortoise with its shell is an important mythological image in many cultures. It is often related to creation myths. In China there is a myth that states that the Chinese script was derived from the 'calligraphy' on the tortoise's shell. The creation myth of my own writing is that it was born out of the unresolved mourning for my father's death. Although it remains my first and preferred form of expression, I have also always been very ambivalent about it. There is a distrust or fear that it might fossilize the lived experiences and turn the mourning into a memorial. As Forest acknowledges, writing gives testimony to our mourning but does not necessarily help us come to terms with it. In order for our mourning to liquefy we have to perform it. Traditional forms of lament such as the Greek *moirológhia* offer a template for how we can perform our mourning.

# Notes


1   Harrison 2003, p. 54.
2   Leader 2008, p. 6.
3   Ibid., p. 31.
4   Ibid., p. 86.
5   Ibid., p. 87.
6   Delecroix and Forest 2015, p. 105: 'Finalement, c'est peut-être cela la littérature: fabriquer des *personas*, des effigies, des personnages—faire le portrait des absents. C'est un art du deuil.'
7   Forest 2004, p. 345: 'impardonnables et pourtant innocents, nous qui sommes vivants.'
8   Delecroix and Forest 2015, p. 101: 'la littérature antique ... exprime non pas la réconciliation du rite mais la protestation du deuil.'
9   Ibid., p. 101: 'le rituel mime et scénographie la douleur, objective socialement la douleur subjective.'
10  Heaney 1966, p. 28.
11  Martel 1996, p. 328.
12  Ibid., p. 95.
13  Ibid., p. 315.
14  Ibid., pp. 133–134.
15  Barnes 2013, p. 68.
16  Porter 2015, p. 103.
17  Ibid., p. 4–5.
18  Ibid., p. 60.
19  Sontag 2017, p. 37.
20  Ibid., p. 41.
21  Ibid., p. 49.
22  Ibid., p. 54.
23  Ibid., p. 47.
24  Ibid., p. 56.
25  Ibid., p. 53.
26  Kitamura 2017, p. 228.
27  Ibid., p. 41.
28  Ibid., pp. 72–73.
29  See also www.rewritingdistance.com.
30  Cixous 1991, p. 38
31  Ibid., p. 52.
32  Keleman 1999, p. 3.
33  Ibid., p. 34.
34  Corradi 1990, p. 72.

# The Greek *moirológhia* as a Template for Performing Mourning

(For Katerina Zakka)
Brave women who survived
Brave women who celebrate
Life by reviving time and again
Their own sorrows to comfort
Others the older you get
The more beatific you are

Singing birds, migrating birds,
Weeping birds, birds of virtue
Who are guarding the trees
To protect their village
The axis mundi of our globe
One day, maybe soon, I will
Fly, too, resurrected
Out of the ashes of your tears
Are born new airs[1]

In the summer of 2000, not long after I had re-lived the mourning of my father's death, I was invited to participate in the first Summer Academy of Theatre organized by the National Theatre of Greece and curated by Eleni Varopoulou. It took place in Monodendri, one of the Zagoria villages north of Ioannina in Epirus, close to the Albanian border. The overall theme of this first edition of the summer academy was 'Ancient chorus and polyphonic expression: contemporary theater work and folk traditions.' I was given the means to bring a team of four people. Apart from myself it included the Belgium-based Italian choreographer Paola Bartoletti and the Dutch-Belgian composer Dick van der Harst, who were both seeking to explore contemporary dance and music based on more traditional forms. The fourth person was the British theater director David Gothard, who had become well acquainted with the Albanian part of the region and its local customs while staging a Shakespearean play there. Our workshop was called 'Rites of separation (death and exile) and union (marriage) as a source for a theatre practice.' Using fragments of Greek tragedy (*Hippolytus* by Euripides in particular) and the choreographic, musical, and theatrical knowledge of the three guest artists, we wanted to research how elements of the local culture could be made relevant in a contemporary performance practice. To help us, local *moirolói* singer Katerina Zakka joined our international group.

Before travelling to Greece, I had studied the musical and oral tradition of the *moirológhia*,[2] the improvised 'songs of fate and mourning' used to commemorate separations from loved ones at funerals, weddings (when the bride leaves her family to go and live with her in-laws, also marking a separation), and in *xenitia* (exile). My starting point had been Loring M. Danforth's anthropological study *The Death Rituals of Rural Greece* (1982). Reality, however, proved much more powerful than anything I had come across in my readings. We worked in a majestic landscape: the wild nature of the Vikos canyon, Europe's largest canyon; the mythical landscape of Dodoni, which includes one of Greece's best-preserved amphitheaters and, according to Greek mythology, is the birthplace of Zeus; and the ruins of a Byzantine monastery, which resemble the landscape of a Tarkovsky movie and where the workshop itself took place.

> My Greek Initiation
> Anche. The beginning. There is
> A laughless rock in the Vikos
> Canyon near Monodendri
> Where I sat to sing my mantra
> A weeping song for a father
> Whose death had too long veiled
> Me but here where eagles still fly
> My tears turned liquid again
> By birds chanting the earth.

Katerina and the other *moirolói* singers who joined the workshop turned out to be powerful old women: semi-professional performers who were able to change register within seconds, lamenting and crying intensely one moment and moving the entire audience to tears, only to joke heartily about their sexual appetite for the young men in our company the next. Eros and Thanatos were sisterly and somatically reunited in the same female bodies and voices.

Normally the *moirológhia* are performed as part of the *kláma*, which literally translates as 'crying' or 'wailing,' but which is the Greek version of a wake, where the body of the deceased is washed and dressed by his or her closest kin. Afterwards it is laid out in an open casket in a room of the house, so that relatives and friends can visit to say their last goodbyes and offer their condolences. During the wake, it is mainly the women who lament.

In the *kláma*, active participation is allowed on basis of either kinship or your own *pónos*. The Greek word *pónos* is difficult to translate. The concept it describes is as complex as the subtle difference between mourning and grief, which I attempted to differentiate in the first chapter. *Pónos* in Greek is always plural. It encompasses pain, grief, suffering, and sorrow. Danforth writes: 'The complex of emotions denoted by the term *ponos* is an expression of the social bonds that tie people together.'[3] Although I have never experienced an actual kláma, I feel that I was allowed to be a privileged witness to the Greek tradition and was able to give testimony on it on the basis of my own *pónos*. In his study *Emotion, Performance & Death Ritual in Inner Mani* (2013), the Greek anthropologist Christos Varvantakis warns against 'subtracting the laments from the mourning context in which they are produced.'[4] But my distance as a stranger to the tradition and the demonstrative nature of Katerina's performance allowed me to grasp the creative and performative potential of this tradition for other contemporary art contexts.

One of the techniques used by the *moirolói* singers is to create a link between the current mourning process and older, similar instances of grief that they have personally experienced. Using many concrete examples from his own fieldwork Varvantakis illustrates how 'the lamenter draws parallels between the present lamented death and her own previous losses' in order 'to position any individual death within a continuum of pain.'[5] In *Dangerous Voices: Women's Laments in Greek Literature* (1992, 1995), Gail Holst-Warhaft mentions the same strategy, describing how professional lamenters invited 'to lament at the funeral of someone they are not close to will deliberately focus on some private suffering to acquire the necessary *ponos* for a performance.'[6] Nikos Menoudakis, a present-day *moirolói* singer from Epirus, explains that practicing lament singing requires identification with another's grief. 'I think the key word is empathy. For us, we recall our own memories of loss and share the grief of the people who ask for consolation with our singing.'[7]

Varvantakis goes on to describe the poetic techniques of the lamenters, 'which include the use of metaphor ..., bodily gesturing and movement, linguistic expression and expression "on the borders" of the linguistic, as with wailing and sobbing—all of which in practice *shape emotion into song*.'[8] The laments are used to both channel and regulate the emotions, holding the space for everyone present so that they can express their emotions but not completely lose control of them. The capacity of the lamenter to maintain a clear singing style and narrative 'refers to the lamenter's ability to regulate, or better, to channel, her emotion into singing.'[9] After being performed, laments become part of an oral history that continues to be remembered and discussed, sometimes for several generations. The difference between a 'good' and a 'bad' lament is the extent to which the proper balance between the expression and the control of emotions has been maintained.

> A good lament performance is expected to wield consistency in its narrative and its performative display through an adept 'handling' of emotion. A bad lament performance is where the narrative drive of the performance is either considered lost or diluted through the lamenter becoming overly 'emotional' and losing control.[10]

Margaret Alexiou was one of the first Greek scholars to study the Greek laments in depth. Her book, *The Ritual Lament in Greek Tradition* (1974, 2002), looks at laments from three distinct periods: antiquity, the Byzantine era, and modern times. In antiquity, the lament in its dramatic form was one of the building blocks of Greek tragedy. In the Byzantine era, it became an important part of the Greek-orthodox church service, in particular Mary's laments for Christ. As part of her research into laments from the modern era, Alexiou conducted field research in different parts of Greece, including in Mani, Epirus and Thessaloniki. Her study focuses on a literary analysis of these laments, i.e., their stylistic and structural characteristics and the different topoi and metaphors used. The themes and conventions she identifies are both ancient and traditional. Their recurrence in today's Greek folkloric laments indicates that they developed out of a single tradition. This is evident not only from the nature of the ideas that are being expressed, but also from the consistency of the expressive and metaphoric formulae used.[11]

As an oral tradition, the *moirológhia* use a formalized, metaphorical language of images and topoi that refer to actual environments and landscapes and allow the singers to easily interact with each other. Alexiou gives an overview of these images and metaphors. Some of them belong to more universal, less localized categories, for example when the opposites of life and death are characterized as an opposition between the 'light of the day/sun' and the 'dark of the night':

> Today there has been a great cry,
> The sun has darkened ...
> There is winter blackness
> And day has turned into night[12]

Another common theme is the notion that the dead have to undertake 'a journey.' In most laments, death is described as 'a journey, either on foot, on Charon's black horse, or by boat to a strange land from which the dead strive to return.'[13] Many of the images are derived from nature, such as for example the common metaphor of the uprooted tree, which is harvested by death:

> For the world is a tree, and we are its fruit,
> and Charos, who is the vintager, gathers its fruit[14]

Others are more specific, referencing elements of a particular topography. Often plants and birds are used to talk about the dead: a cypress, for instance, can represent a deceased man, while an orange tree or a lemon tree may stand for a woman. Or a partridge can represent a young woman and an eagle a young man. Holst-Warhaft discusses how placing the deceased in a concrete landscape, often heightened by the use of place names and toponyms, also keeps the memory of the dead person alive. She calls it 'a device for anchoring the nebulous dead in the concrete surroundings of the survivor.'[15]

The *moirológhia* are by nature theatrical. One particular dramatic strategy is that the singer addresses the absent person and temporarily lends them her voice to answer back. A widow can thus talk to her husband, a mother to her married daughter, a corpse to its own 'tired body.' Danforth also stresses that the *moirológhia* allow the living 'to carry on a "conversation" with the dead.'[16] This 'reality-sustaining conversation' keeps the deceased alive for a little while longer, 'at least in the sense that the living continue to interact with him after his death.'[17]

As part of her ongoing research on how new communication technologies and social media influence our social skills, MIT psychologist Sherry Turkle tells the story of a Rabbi's sermon on Yom Kippur during Yizkor, the service of mourning for the dead. Mirroring the dialogue that unfolds between the *moirológhia* and the deceased, the Rabbi in Turkle's story talks about the importance of being in dialogue with the dead. He suggests that 'we have four things to say to them: I'm sorry. Thank you. I forgive you. I love you.'[18] These are among the core messages that appear in almost all laments. (It should be said here that not only is it good advice to make amends with the dead, but also with the living.)

The relationship between the *moirológhia's* leading voice and the chorus is characterized by an antiphonic, dialogic structure: the leading voice is reinforced by the other women who polyphonically hum or cry along. In her study *The Last Word: Women, Death, and Divination in Inner Mani* (1991), Nadia Seremetakis attempts 'to systematize the performative contexts of lamenting.'[19] She offers a detailed discussion of this 'ethics of antiphony,' in which a chorus of *moirolyistres* generates antiphonic responses to the *koriféa*, 'the soloist in pain.' The leading *koriféa* role will be passed on to several women during the course of the wake. The passing on of the role of the soloist among the chorus is described with the words 'to give' and 'to take' and is often accompanied by a gesture or a touch (such as taking the hand of the next lamenter). Antiphonic responses include 'singing the refrains, such as doubling the last word of the verse or the last verse of the lament, and stylized sobbing that occurs simultaneously with and in counterpoint to the singing of the *koriféa*.'[20] Seremetakis states that the antiphonic interaction between soloist and chorus is necessary 'to attain the proper emotional intensity.'[21] At its core is an alternation between sobbing and discourse, between language and non-language: 'The sob occupies a pivotal position in this movement from nonlanguage to language.' It combines 'the acoustic dynamics of heavy breathing, breathlessness, and syllabic prolongation as emotional intensifiers.'[22] Seremetakis continues:

> The penetration of language by stylized sobbing takes the acoustic form of microtonal variations and accidental harmonics which infiltrate each note and each word of the lament. The mourner sings with more than one voice and in more than one pitch at the same time. Through the sob, the singer fractures the musical tone, propels it into the space of the kláma in a polyphony of pain.[23]

This polyphony thus includes both the improvised singing of the soloist and the antiphonic responses of the chorus, which are

punctuated by stylized sobbing, screaming, and by improvised monologues in prose. Visually, they are accompanied by 'the multiple corporeal gestures of soloist and chorus.'[24] Holst-Warhaft draws attention to the intake of breath as another element in this non-verbal repertoire of sounds and gestures: 'Singers of dramatic or plaintive songs from opera to blues will use their breath for heightened emotional effect.'[25] She goes on to explain that in Greek culture (as in many other cultures) breath is associated with soul and spirit. As a result, the musical expression of grief is often assigned to wind instruments such as the double-pipe or *aulós*, which are frequently mentioned in elegies from the classical period. Other examples include the legend of Pan and Syrinx, where a wind instrument appears as a form of expression of amorous grief, and the laments of Epirus, where the clarinet plays an important role.

Finally, the antiphonic structure of the *moirológhia* also functions as a mnemonic device. The repetition of part of the verses by different voices makes it easier to remember them and also allows the individual mourning to be 'reconstructed as a collective oral history'[26] that is kept alive in the community. In her book *For the Living and the Dead* (2010), the Canadian anthropologist Elizabeth Wickett describes how the funerary laments of Upper Egypt, the *idid*, are built on a similar 'interaction between the principal lamenter, her respondent, the bereaved and the consoling chorus,' and how 'emotion is incarnated and released in the meshing of voices.'[27] Seremetakis concludes that the dialogic, antiphonic structure of the laments is not so much an aesthetic device but rather a reflection of 'the social structure of mortuary ritual,' and 'a political strategy that organizes the relation of women to male-dominated institutions.'[28] Both Seremetakis and Wickett argue that the *moirológhia* and the *idid* create transgressive sanctuaries for women that not only allow them to express their grief, but also give them opportunities to talk about, comment on, and critique dominant male institutions. The official, orthodox religion has developed its own rituals of mourning, which are frequently in opposition to the *moirológhia* and which seek to displace the older traditions. Seremetakis writes: 'The displacement of the mourning singing by the Byzantine chant encodes a confrontation of two musical cultures, which in turn expresses the historical divergences between two institutions—one local, oral, and improvised, the other metropolitan and textual.'[29]

The early studies of the *moirológhia* were conducted by literary scholars or anthropologists who concentrated on textual evidence. Only recently have the laments' musical characteristics begun to attract scholarly attention as well. The ethno-musicologist Luc Charles-Dominique, for example, has compared several Western musical traditions that primarily express emotions such as grief, pain, and suffering, including the *moirológhia*, rebetiko, fado and tango. All these musical forms embrace the principle of 'discontinuity,' which also characterizes the human mourning process. Discontinuity is present in these musical genres on the levels of melody, harmony, rhythm, and timbre (both instrumental and vocal). 'The music breaks apart, like the voice does under the weight of the emotions.'[30] More specifically, discontinuity is achieved by employing certain techniques: songs are punctuated by cries and sighs, and volumes and registers change frequently (for example when the singer moves from a chest voice to a head voice or vice versa). What these musical expressions imply is 'the idea of stepping over a threshold, not only on the level of expressing the suffering, but also in the musical form itself.'[31] In order for this musical discontinuity to have an emotional impact, it has to remain unpredictable. A pitch break which interrupts the melodic line, also has to give the impression that it wasn't rehearsed or planned in order to suggest the loss of control and emotions breaking out, through mere sound.[32]

In the Epirus region, the *moirológhia* have developed into a genuine musical genre similar to Portuguese fado or the blues. They have become part of a larger musical culture, in which individual musicians have created their own instrumental versions of certain songs. These are also recorded and performed outside of the specific context of funeral rites. When the American music producer and musicologist Christopher C. King 'accidentally' discovered the genre, chancing on a collection of old 78 records by the Epirotic musician Kitsos Harisiadis in a second-hand shop in Istanbul, he set out on 'an odyssey' to discover 'Europe's oldest surviving folk music.' King's quest is recorded in the documentary film *While You Live, Shine* (2018) by the Irish director Paul Duane. He has also written a book about it, *Lament from Epirus* (2018), and re-released a series of the original recordings.

The instrumental versions of the *moirológhia* are mostly performed on the violin or clarinet, whose high pitches resemble the *aulós* (reed-pipe) of antiquity: 'a public and a private musical

*memento mori*, it is a calculated wailing through an instrument.'[33] They are traditionally performed at the beginning and the end of the local *panegyria*, village celebrations featuring music and dance in honor of local saints or religious events in the Greek orthodox calendar. 'During the *panegyria* the *mirológi* bookends the celebration: it is the alpha and the omega.'[34]

As a musicologist, King offers valuable insights into the characteristics of the *moirológhia*. He distinguishes two key motifs: ostinato and a descending glissando. 'An ostinato is a phrase, passage or motif that is persistently repeated throughout a tune.' Individual musicians will develop personal signatures that can be recognized by anyone familiar with the genre.

> The descending glissando of this region is a sliding ornament, either subtle or hyperbolic, from a higher note in a scale ... to a lower register note. The elision is typically languid, as if all the blood is being drained from the instrument while playing.[35]

The *moirológhia* of Epirus use the pentatonic scale, as does the blues. The pentatonic scale contains five pitches per octave that can be combined in 'endless permutations.' 'What appears on the outside as a limited musical vocabulary can contain within itself the infinite elements needed to tell a nuanced story.'[36]

During my fellowship at the International Research Center 'Interweaving Performance Cultures', when I was working on the first draft of this book, I had an exchange with the voice coach and scholar Tara McAllister-Viel. After listening to one of my field recordings of Katerina Zakka, Tara analyzed it and created a vocal profile of the singer. This vocal profile describes the use of breath, resonance, pitch, the articulations of individual phonemes (vowels and consonants but also gibberish), and the 'text,' i.e., the meaning derived from the combination of sound and words. Tara also noted the repetitive ostinato and the descending glissando, but added a series of other meaningful observations: Katerina's *moirolói* starts with a strong initial tonal center and ends in a yelp. Her breath is often made audible. The timbre of her voice frequently and quickly shifts from a chest voice to a head voice and back. The vibrational qualities of the vowels—the contrast between 'a' and 'i,' for example—are heightened to increase their emotional resonance. In order to achieve this, words are often split in unusual places so that the vowels are lengthened.

The Greek singer and music therapist Xanthoula Dakovanou, who is also the musical director of the dance production *Lamenta* (see also chapter 'Laments as a Collective Form of Witnessing'), discusses in her essay 'Quand l'âme chante: La voix mélodique et son pouvoir affectif' (When the soul sings: The Melodic Voice and its Emotional Power, 2012) how 'the waves of vocalized ornaments translate the affective vibrations in a more direct and truthful way than words.'[37] She continues to explain that this is one of the reasons why in a lot of oriental music the text is often deconstructed or even abandoned to improvise on non-sensical words such as for instance the word *aman* (Oh God, what happened!) in a lot of Greek and Turkish music.[38]

Tara also points out that the use of the breath and the sob should not be seen as being in opposition to the narrative elements of the lament: there is no binary division between non-language and language, nor between the laments' verbal and non-verbal elements. The audible breath might be used to articulate the recurrent 'ohhs' and 'ahhs,' which are both verbal and meaningful. 'The placement of the sob punctuates and augments the message of the lament and the representation in performance of a real sob has both metaphoric and aesthetic meaning.'[39] Tara considers all the vocal expressions of the lament to be on a form/function spectrum.

While the musical and textual structure of the *moirológhia* is highly codified, it leaves ample room for improvisation, enabling the singer to stay in the present and enter into a dialogue with the deceased. James Wilce's book *Crying Shame: Metaculture, Modernity, and the Exaggerated Death of Lament* (2009) is one of very few comparative studies looking at laments in different cultures. He includes the Greek *moirológhia*, the Irish *caoineadh*, Finnish *itkuvirsi*, Bangla *bilap*, and laments from the Shia Muslim traditions.[40] Wilce states that in most of these traditions, the 'formulae for lyrical and musical performance are *traditionally transmitted*,' but must also 'appear as something new—contextualized to some extent to fit the particular death.' Lament performers are like jazz musicians who constantly 're-compose' the standards in a jam session. 'Local genres of lament are re-created or renewed in each performance.'[41]

The other place where the *moirológhia* are traditionally performed is in the graveyard. In his study Danforth describes how in the 1970s the women of a small, rural village in Northern Greece would visit the graves of their deceased relatives for an hour every day for five years after the funeral. There they would musically interact with them, using the *moiróloi* form:

> The site of this interaction, the place where the conversation between the living and the dead takes place, is the grave. ... Not only is the grave a kind of house or home for the deceased, it is also a second house or second home (*dheftero spiti*) for the bereaved woman, who spends so much time there visiting and caring for her dead relative.[42]

As a result, references to graves and tombstones feature prominently in many of the laments. These references may become more descriptive and specific as the laments become more personalized. In the graveyard, individual dialogues are woven into a chorus of mourning voices that not only commemorates the dead but also offers a means of support for the women among each other. They compare experiences and comment on daily events. Their individual stories are integrated into a collective canon that leaves room for individual experience:

> These laments constitute a public language, a cultural code, for the expression of grief. They provide the bereaved with a set of shared symbols ... which enables them not only to organize their experience of death in a culturally meaningful way but also to articulate it in a socially approved manner. Women singing laments are communicating in a symbolic language and in the context of a public performance.[43]

Danforth's analysis of Greek funeral rites and the *moirológhia* in particular draws on the classic tripartite structure of 'rites of passage,' as they were originally described by Arnold van Gennep and further developed by anthropologists such as Claude Lévi-Strauss and Clifford Geertz. This classic structure always begins with a binary opposition, such as the one between life and death. Then, a third concept is added: a mediating term that defines the in-between state, passage, or transition from one to the other. The theory proposes that all rites follow a linear sequence, in which a relatively stable 'before' state is followed by an unstable, liminal in-between state, which in turn leads to a stable 'after' state.

<blockquote>

In the rich and moving tradition of Greek funeral laments, marriage, xenitia, plants, food, water, poison, tears, and birds are all associated with the attempt to mediate the opposition between life and death, to move from an awareness of this opposition to its resolution. Each of these images attempts to provide a means of overcoming the contradiction between life and death, but this is an impossibility. The attempt is doomed to failure.[44]

</blockquote>

As is clear from the stories of personal mourning processes described in chapter one, the reality of grief is often more discontinuous and stretches out over longer periods of time, during which the grieving person re-visits liminal states of mourning several times over. Recent studies from the field of trauma treatment have used the infinity symbol as a metaphor for this process, identifying its two parts as a 'trauma vortex' and a 'healing vortex.' Both parts need to be visited over and over again in safe ways (i.e., through small, contained experiences) in order to process 'stuck' or frozen emotions. It is a process that resembles the peeling of an onion, as each layer reveals another, deeper layer underneath. My personal experience of mourning very much bears this out.

Today, we have detailed analyses of the *moirológhia* from both a textual and a musical perspective, but what is almost entirely missing in the current research is an analysis of the physical language that accompanies and, in some cases, embodies the wailing. References to physicality are extremely sporadic and sparse. Both Wickett and Seremetakis mention that the singing, crying and screaming of the lamenters is accompanied by specific corporeal gestures and movements. Seremetakis goes on to describe how 'women represent the violence of death through their own bodies' and how 'this corporeal mimesis of death' involves 'the transformation of their bodies into a text of disorder,' which on occasion leads them to strip off clothes or pull their hair and can go as far as 'the scarring of flesh.'[45]

<blockquote>

The *moiroloyistra* (mourner) creates the center with her physical presence by molding her body through gestures, caresses, and improvised discourses around the space of the corpse. All these are dramatic expressions of an ethic of care and of tending the dead. Mourning necessitates

</blockquote>

touching and caressing the dead, leaning over the dead with tender gestures as if talking to a sleeping person.[46]

Alexiou explicitly compares the movements to a dance:

The archaeological and literary evidence, taken together, makes it clear that lamentation involved movement as well as wailing and singing. Since each movement was determined by a pattern of ritual ... the scene must have resembled a dance, sometimes slow and solemn, sometimes wild and ecstatic.'[47]

As a dance dramaturg I am particularly interested in this embodiment of the lament. In the following chapters I will describe some of the creation processes of contemporary dance pieces that I have been involved in and that have drawn on the traditions of lament.

Two years after the workshop in Greece, Dick van der Harst and I returned to Ioannina to exchange with Katerina once more, to study her art in more detail. As a retired teacher, Katerina had begun to write down the lyrics of her songs, which until then had been preserved through a predominantly oral tradition. She sang them to us so that Dick could note down their improvised musical patterns. Out of this research, Dick developed a theatrical concert, *Dakrisména Póulia (Weeping Birds)*, which was produced by Muziek Lod in Ghent. In it he combined Katerina's traditional *moirológhia* with some of the songs he had written for Eric De Volder's theater production *Zwarte Vogels in de bomen* (Black Birds in the Trees) which were performed by the soprano Katelijne Van Laethem. The concert premiered at the 2003 edition of the Time Festival, a city-wide festival curated by the Colombian theater director and anthropologist Enrique Vargas around the subject of the *Ars Moriendi* or art of dying.

One of the main goals of the *moirológhia* is to perform mourning and elicit tears as 'material signs of the liquefaction'[48] of grief. Danforth describes in detail how tears can mediate between the apparent opposites of life and death. For the mourner they are bitter, representing the poison of grief leaving the body, while for the deceased, they bring relief: 'Tears are associated with death in this world but with life in the underworld.'[49]

> Strangers, kinsmen, and all you who grieve, come near.
> Say a few words to me and shed a few tears.
> So that the tears become a cool spring, a lake, an ocean,
> And flood down into the underworld,
> So that the unwashed can wash, and the thirsty can drink.[50]

Tears are an affective expression of a range of emotions, spanning everything from sadness to joy. Our attitude toward tears has shifted throughout history and is highly dependent on cultural contexts, as Anne Vincent-Buffault's study *Histoire des larmes* (*The History of Tears*, 1986) illustrates. There are also marked differences between genders. On a physical level, tears are material signs of physiological processes in which the body releases fluids as a result of pain. Many movement practitioners have experienced tears flowing as a result of a moment of physical release from tension or strain. Fluidity and movement are signs of healthy somatic processes. It is when the flow is interrupted, blocked, or comes to a complete standstill over a long period that we fall ill, either physically or psychologically.

Traditional laments liquefy the emotions of grief in order to restore energy flow and vitality. How they do this resembles the somatic therapy processes that the American clinical psychologist Peter A. Levine has developed to treat trauma.[51] Levine uses the concept of renegotiation, which is 'completely different from cathartic "traumatic reliving."'[52] Rather than reliving the traumatic memories and their emotions, Levine's approach focuses on 'feelings accessed through body awareness.'[53] The main tools for this are 'the twin sisters of awareness and embodiment,'[54] which Levine's therapy aims to support through 'the vital balancing act between expression and restraint.'[55] The same balancing act is performed by the laments: their codified language negotiates control and loss of control through artifice.

In her book *Grief Works*, Julia Samuel describes how experiences of grief 'sit in the body' and how 'people often talk about is as "a knot" or as "a block" in their throat or stomach.'[56] In *The New Black*, Daniel Leader writes that 'physical symptoms and somatizations would occur when mourning was blocked or unsuccessful.'[57] He references an older, influential study by Geoffrey Gorer, *Death, Grief and Mourning* (1965), which introduced the widespread notion that the decline of mourning rituals such as laments increased during periods when there were too many deaths to be mourned properly. The immediate aftermath of World War I is one such example. Leader explains that the somatic symptoms and physical illnesses caused by blocked, unsuccessful mourning often flare up on meaningful anniversaries or dates connected to the original loss. Data from large-scale hospital studies in the US confirm this hypothesis, which is also supported by anecdotal evidence. Leader mentions the case of the writer Nikolai Gogol, who died by suicide through starvation at the age of forty-three, the same age at which his father had succumbed to an illness. In this context, Danforth's study positions the Greek *moirológhia* as an important and necessary somatic release from harmful grief:

> With crying and singing, a knot (*komvos*) leaves one's throat, one is lightened (*elafreni*), and one feels cool (*dhrosizete*). When a woman visits the graveyard and cries, ponos, anxiety and poison all leave her system. A woman performs the necessary rites of passage and cares for the graves of the dead "in order to get everything out of her system" (*ya na xespasi*). These visits to the graveyard are one of the few opportunities for the cathartic outburst of emotion (*xespasma*) available to a woman in mourning.[58]

In his study of the music of Epirus, Christopher King concludes that the 'music's preeminent purpose in northwestern Greece is deceptively simple: it heals. The musical "laying on of hands" is therapeutic and curative to the individual and the village.'[59] Unlike Philippe Forest (see second chapter), I do believe in the healing potential of performing one's grief. In her contribution to *Rethinking Tragedy* (2008), the feminist theologian Kathleen M. Sands explicitly links 'the tragic' with 'the traumatic' experienced in loss. Whereas traumas are 'black holes' which 'manifest themselves as gaps or silence,' tragedy, as an aesthetic form, creates 'a ritual space where the trauma, rather than being silently re-enacted, is solemnly voiced and lamented.'[60] Through this voicing, which is a process of re-embodiment, the seeming fatality of the experience of loss is transformed. It acquires a form that can be acted upon.

Harrison extensively references and quotes the Italian anthropologist Ernesto de Martino, who in *Morte e pianto rituale* (Death and Ritual Lament, 1958) studied the mourning rituals and laments of the interior of Basilicata in southern Italy. As de

Martino points out, 'it is precisely the impersonal character of the stereotypes that make possible an interpersonal participation in the lament ... which would be wholly inconceivable under a strictly personal regime of mourning.'[61] Harrison eloquently rephrases this and concludes: 'As ritual lament submits the emotive spontaneity of grief to impersonal forms of expression, it opens the possibility of an interpersonal nexus of participation and thereby gives grief a voice.'[62]

The physical exteriorization of grief through lamenting is a necessary part of the rites of separation. It allows the mourner to stay connected to the deceased for some time but eventually also facilitates their reintegration into society. As the Roland Barthes quote at the beginning of the first chapter indicates, our Western society has suppressed these external rituals (with some noteworthy exceptions such as the Greek example). It has interiorized mourning, which carries serious risks of psychological, physical, and energetic blockages in the body. Through cyclically revisiting one's mourning, grief is eventually exteriorized and exorcised, resulting in the loosening of negative energy or energy blockages. In the process, personal experiences are integrated into a larger collective tradition and can become material for a creative practice. Artistic practices can open up spaces for articulating and renegotiating the pain of loss.

# Notes

1 When not referenced differently, verses like these are my own. I am used to write them as a different way of keeping a diary to remember certain events or encounters.

2 Following most scholars on the topic (Alexiou 1974, 2002, Danforth 1982, Seremetakis 1991, Holst-Warhaft 1992, 1995 and Varvantakis 2013), I follow the phonetic transliteration of the Greek characters, with *moirolói* for the singular and *moirológhia* as the plural form.

3 Danforth 1982, p. 141.

4 Varvantakis 2013, p. 93.

5 Ibid., p. 121.

6 Holst-Warhaft 1992, 1995, pp. 109–110.

7 Menoudakis in Simon 2017, p. 202.

8 Varvantakis, p. 162.

9 Ibid., p. 102.

10 Ibid., p. 161.

11 See Alexiou 1974, 2002, p. 184.

12 Lament from Mani, quoted in Alexiou 1974, 2002, p. 168–169:
> Σήμερα ἐγίγνη ἀλαλαγμός,
> ὁ ἥλιος ἐσκουτείνιασε …
> Σκοτάδι χειμωνιάτικο
> κι ἡμέρα νύχτα ἔγινε.

13 Holst-Warhaft 1992, 1995, p. 55.

14 Lament from Epirus, quoted by Alexiou 1974, 2002, p. 201:
> Γιατί ὁ κόσμος εἶν' δεντρί, καί
> μεῖς τ ' ὀπωρικό του,
> κι ὁ Χάρος, πού εἶν' ο τρυγητής,
> μαζώνει τον καρπόν του.

15 Holst-Warhaft 1992, 1995, p. 36.

16 Danforth 1982, p. 117.

17 Ibid., p. 127.

18 Turkle 2011, p. 304.

19 Seremetakis 1991, p. IX.

20 Ibid., pp. 99–100.

21 Ibid., p. 100.

22 Ibid., p. 117.

23 Ibid., p. 118.

24 Ibid., p. 106.

25 Holst-Warhaft 1992, 1995, p. 70.

26 Seremetakis 1991, p. 105.

27 Wickett 2010, p. 100.

28 Seremetakis 1991, p. 100.

29 Ibid., p. 165.

30 Charles-Dominique 2011, p. 85: 'La musique se brise, à l'image de la voix sous le coup de l'émotion.'

31 Ibid., p. 90: 'l'idée de franchissement d'un seuil, non seulement dans le niveau de douleur à exprimer mais surtout dans son mode d'expression même.'

32 The latter insight was offered to me by my colleague, the voice coach and scholar Tara McAllister-Viel, who specialized, among other things, in the Korean musical drama of *p'ansori*. See also further.

33 King 2018, p. 71.

34 Ibid., p. 218.

35 Ibid., p. 100.

36 Ibid., p. 157.

37 Dakovanou 2012, 2013, p. 24: 'C'est comme si les ondes des ornements vocaux traduisaient les vibrations affectives de façon plus immédiate et fidèle que les mots.'

38 Ibid., p. 26.

39 From a personal message from Tara McAllister-Viel, January 6th, 2021.

40 Although Wilce's study contains many interesting examples from very different cultures, his meta-discourse on how modernity and post-modernity deal with 'tradition' frequently takes precedent, sidelining the actual case studies.

41 Wilce 2009, p. 174–175.

42 Danforth 1982, p. 133.

43 Ibid., p. 73–74.

44 Ibid., p. 115.

45 Seremetakis 1991, p. 74.

46 Ibid., p. 96.

47 Alexiou 1974, 2002, p. 6.

48 Seremetakis 1991, p. 115.

49 Danforth 1982, p. 110.

50 Traditional lament, quoted by Danforth 1982, pp. 110–111:
> Γιά ἐλᾶτε ξένοι καί δικοί καί ὅλοι
> οἱ πικραμένοι,
> κι ἀπό 'να λόγο πέστε μου κι ἀπό
> 'να δάκρυ χύστε,
> να γένη λίμνη καί γιαλός, να
> γένη κρύα βρύση,
> να πάρη τόν κατήφορο νά πάει
> στόν Κάτω Κόσμο,
> για να νιφτοῦν οἱ ἄνιφτοι, να
> πιοῦν οἱ διψασμένοι.

51 Levine's therapy is called Somatic Experiencing.

52 Levine 2010, p. 184.

53 Ibid., p. 345.

54 Ibid., p. 313.

55 Ibid., p. 321.

56 Samuel 2017, p. 229.

57 Leader 2008, p. 95.

58 Danforth 1982, p. 144.

59 King 2018, p. 250. See also King's TEDx talk, held in Athens in 2019 on 'The healing music of Epirus': The Healing Music of Epirus | Christopher C. King | TEDxAthens.

60 Sands 2008, p. 83.

61 Harrison 2003, p. 59.

62 Ibid., p. 62.

# Laments in Contemporary Art

In her introduction to *Mourning Sex* (1997), Peggy Phelan states that 'theatre and performance respond to a psychic need to rehearse for loss, and especially for death.'[1] Similarly, it is my personal conviction that a large part of past and present artistic creation can be understood as a dialogue between the artist and the ghosts of the dead. The liminal state of an as yet unresolved mourning process—which can be both individual and collective—is often better expressed through artistic expressions than through psychological terminology.

The five subsections of this chapter are thematically defined. In section one, I focus on the dialogical nature of contemporary art practices that deal with personal losses and individual mourning processes. In section two, the focus is on more collective mourning rituals and how they invite communities to witness these losses. Section three presents contemporary examples of laments that are not only used to dialogue with the dead but also to communicate with loved ones who are absent because of migration or exile. Section four deals with the very specific form of mourning that occurs when we grieve for the unrealized potential of a child's unlived life, including that of an unborn child. Finally, section five addresses the very recent phenomenon of lamenting not just the losses of the past, but also the loss of a future. This particularly affects younger generations of artists, who have a sense that their future is threatened by an accumulation of crises in the world.

As I have already indicated in the introduction to this book, the field of artistic practices that could be considered to be forms of contemporary laments because they deal with loss and mourning is extremely wide and continues to expand. I will therefore concentrate on art works that I have a personal connection with. In some cases, this is because I contributed to their creation process, in others it is because I know the artists personally, and in yet others it is simply because I discovered these works at a meaningful moment in my own journey. The collection of laments that I present here is thus a very subjective and even idiosyncratic selection. Not all of them would even be considered laments in the strictest sense, in which a lament is defined as a 'combination of three elements— tuneful, texted weeping.'[2] I hope that both the uniqueness and diversity of the chosen examples will create enough 'cracks in the wall' for readers to add their own experiences and examples.

# Laments to Dialogue with Those Who Are Absent

> Once, ritual lament would have been chanted;
> Women would have been paid to beat their breasts
> And howl for you all night, when all is silent.
> Where can we find such customs now? So many
> Have long since disappeared or been disowned.
> That's what you had to come for: to retrieve
> The lament that we omitted. Can you hear me?[3]

Originally, I was fascinated by the dramatic and theatrical nature of the *moirológhia*: the singers address the dead and the absent and then lend them their own voices to answer back. By doing so, they offer them a second chance at life. In the examples below I describe a number of diverse artistic practices from different disciplines and mediums that I consider to be forms of contemporary laments. Like the *moirológhia*, they establish a triangulation between the artists, their audiences, and the absent persons they dialogue with.

When I was still regularly working in Toronto, I would always stay with the Canadian painter Jane Martin. Her husband had died after being diagnosed with a fatal brain tumor before we first met. All through his agony, Jane took Polaroids of him and jotted down his often strange, but poetic, utterances. A few years later she began painting a series of miniature portraits based on these Polaroids, called *Something Happened* (2008). Each of the portraits has one of her husband utterances as a title. Most of the portraits hang in a small private room where she retreats 'to meditate in an ongoing dialogue with him.' Some of the portraits were later shown as part of a group exhibition in the Art Gallery of Ontario, with the title *The Matter of Loss* (2009).

My close friend and artistic partner, the Canadian choreographer Lin Snelling, also performed her mourning, for her mother Eva Snelling. It was a personal, artistic ritual. Eva was born in November and so in 2015, the year following her mother's death, Lin went into the studio for half an hour each day at 7.30 am to improvise a dance. 'The dance followed a simple ritual of beginning on the floor and continuing from there, followed by writing and drawing with eyes closed: as a mapping of sensations, experienced while dancing.'[4] These dances were antiphonic in how they responded to words given to Lin by friends and relatives. Some of these words were: scar(f), loss, prayer, memory, serendipitous, path, epiphany. The resulting notebook—*an endingbeginning*—was offered as a gift to everyone who contributed to her ritual.

Day 4. The word 'loss,' given by Tedi:

> I am born of loss
> You, my mother, convinced by someone else,
> That birth would solve the loss of the death
> And so, I am born of loss
> Today so many times
> My hands, my hands, my hands
> Your hands, your hands, your hands
> My face, your face
> My belly, your belly
> My heart, your heart
> My loss ... you
> Loss and found, loss and find, loss and feel
> Accepting you, and the wonder of our constant sparring
> These arguments you gave me, the love to fight
> To fight for my own voice, to fight for my own freedom
> You sewed clothes for me to wear
> I grew and grew, you kept sewing
> Hands making clothes
> You watched me grow
> Your love for making things
> To sew words, word, love
> Love you sew, so.[5]

Lin's antiphonic writing, in which she dialogues with the words of consolation offered by her friends and with her mother's absence/presence, perfectly illustrates one of Judith Butler's central arguments in 'Violence, Mourning, Politics' (one of the essays in her book *Precarious Life*): 'the attachment to "you" is part of what composes who "I" am. If I lose you ... then I not only mourn the loss, but I become inscrutable to myself. Who "am" I, without you?'[6]

Lin's next work was an even more explicit dialogue between her mother and her. In *EVA* (2017), she focuses on the clothes that she inherited after her mother's death, as well as on the clothes that her mother sewed for her. These clothes not only create a material link between the two women but also clearly demonstrate how a large part of Lin's artistic identity was formed by her mother.

*EVA* is a very intimate performance, set in the costume atelier of the theater department of the University of Alberta, where Lin teaches. Lin uses a recording of an actual conversation

she had with her mother about the clothes she made. 'Hello, my name is Eva Snelling. I started sewing for every event I went to.' The recording was given to three musicians (Jérémi Roy, David Ryshpan, and Michael Reinhart) who independently from each other improvised an accompaniment to it. The individual tracks were then randomly uploaded into a recording program and mixed by Reinhart with the original voice track.

While the audience is listening to her mother speaking, Lin enters the space, gently touching and activating some of the clothes that are draped onto mannequins. Her performance is mostly composed of everyday actions, performed in a slow meditative rhythm. She rearranges the mannequins, places a set of dolls' clothes on a table; she knits, shows a picture of herself as a three-year-old in the 'little white dress' her mother made for her; she dresses, and undresses. These actions are alternated with more choreographed sections, including a falling sequence and a rhythmic, percussive dance to live music. All of Lin's movements and actions are in sync with the voice recording. 'It was her voice, on tape, that created something very powerful.'[7] At one point in the recording, Lin's mother asks her: 'What dress do you remember that I made you that stands out in your memory?' The question allows Lin to take over the dialogue and start recounting her own memories and stories that she associates with the various garments. As a memento mori, the clothes act as an interface between two voices and two generations. The past of her memories and the present of the performance come together in one moment, celebrating their interdependency within the symbolic space of the sewing atelier. Lin speaks:

> This is a room for making. Many things have been made here. It takes time, expertise, skills, luck, a bit of drama and patience, a lot of patience, planning, love. They say good clothing breathes. One can say the same about a performance. It is alive. I think that clothing is still alive, even if the people are dead. Because when it was made, somebody was alive.[8]

Mother and daughter both identify with the art of making, whether it be a dress or a dance. The performance ends like it started, slowly fading out, with Lin embodying her mother's daily actions at the sewing machine and rearranging the clothes on the mannequins.

Another one of my colleagues, the Flemish performing arts curator Barbara Raes, decided to reorient her professional career and practice, after a period of deep exhaustion that obliged her to take a year out, 'doing nothing.' She went to the UK to train as funeral celebrant with the organization *Green Fuse* in the Devon town of Totnes. As part of her training, she observed and analyzed more than eighty funerals, using her experience in the performing arts to better understand the dramaturgy of these rituals of 'saying goodbye.' When she returned to Belgium, she obtained a research position at KASK arts college in Ghent and developed the project *Open End* (2015–2018), in which architecture and healthcare students worked together in an interdisciplinary context to design 'new mental and physical spaces for farewell rituals.'[9]

To complement this more theoretical research, she founded the organization *Beyond the Spoken*,[10] which commissions artists to create rituals that address 'unacknowledged loss.' Unacknowledged losses are 'the little funerals we encounter in our lives' such as surgery, changing schools or jobs, giving birth, getting an abortion, or divorcing, all of which are 'moments of transition, which we do not acknowledge enough, although we actually want and need them to be seen.'[11]

The new rituals designed by *Beyond the Spoken* want to raise awareness of the energetic ups and downs of the mourning process. Barbara describes this energetic process as an S-curve that starts with low energy. Mourners need to be grounded and their energy brought up to a higher level before they can address their sadness and say their goodbyes. This in turn results in a downward energy trend. Toward the end of the ritual, the energy needs to be brought up again, 'to make the situation more acceptable and lighter. To achieve healing, it is necessary to go through all the phases of this S-curve.'[12] The design of the ritual, together with a person accompanying it, 'holding the space,' allows for this S-flow to happen. The people for whom the rituals are designed are most of the time conscious and ready to let go. The ritual is designed to mark the transition and support them in both saying goodbye and moving on.

Capitalizing on her previous networks in the performing arts, Barbara has also curated a series of projects and festivals that explore how art and rituals can address the topic of 'unacknowl-edged loss.' They include the 2019 *amen & beyond* program for the arts center Vooruit in Ghent, which she curated together with the musician Colin Van Eeckhout; the research block *unfolding fields of interaction with health, life, loss and death* for DASarts in

Amsterdam (2016); *U-Loss* for HAU, Berlin (2017 and 2020) and Kaaitheater, Brussels (2019), and the entire 2018 edition of the TAZ Festival in Ostend. For each of the *U-Loss* projects, Barbara led a group of artists from various disciplines and cultural backgrounds in designing their own rituals. In the beginning of the process, the group would be immersed in a series of experiences such as visiting a crematorium or lying in a coffin. They would also talk to and be nurtured by undertakers, palliative nurses, or Zen masters. The personal rituals they developed afterwards, and which were eventually shared with an audience, are described as 'artistic, but not art; theatrical, not theater; therapeutic, not therapy; playful, not a game; time-out-of time, not time-out. We prepare, we don't produce.'[13] One of the participants, the Gabonese artist Nathalie Bikoro, had experienced both a miscarriage and the loss of family members at the hands of her country's post-colonial regime. She stressed the importance of these new rituals: 'When you allow mourning and burials into your life, your whole body changes.'[14]

One of Barbara's most successful projects is the performance ritual *Zon dag kind* (Sun day child), which she designed for the TAZ festival and supports children who have experienced a traumatic loss. In the ritual, a child is taken on a night-time fishing boat trip. Just before dawn, it is woken up and invited by an actress and a musician to sing a song for the sun to rise again on the horizon. The ritual was specifically designed to give the child an intimate experience, accompanied by just one caretaker on the boat. But as it was repeated for a different child every day of the festival, the audiences gathering on the quay to welcome the boat back from its liminal journey grew larger and larger, making it an event for the community as well as an individual journey.

Barbara's research project at KASK allowed her to connect with other artists working on initiatives in the field of ritual and loss. One of them is the Flemish stage and costume designer Valentine Kempynck. With her piece *BANKSJE* (Small bench), Valentine revitalized an old mourning ritual from the rural West-Flanders region.[15] When someone dies in one of the local farms, two bricks are taken from the walls of the house. One is broken into two parts and the other one is fixed on top of the two halves with cement, creating a small, improvised bench. This bench is then affixed to the top of the roof. There are technical and functional reasons for doing this, such as the desire to protect the more fragile parts of the roof against the fierce winds and storms that are common in the

Lowlands. But the practice also creates a psychological space for the mourners and a literal space for the deceased, who is expected to come and visit the house, resting on the 'small bench.'

Valentine began creating *BANKSJES* outside of the region where they originated. She also created them for new contexts, including for individuals who were dealing with losses such as an abortion, divorce, or a tragic death. She would go into communities and guide them in creating and installing their own 'small benches': one was built by the pupils of a school where someone had died by suicide and another was created by refugees in a camp in Calais and installed on top of their improvised communal space. The process of collectively building and affixing the bench was often spread out over many days and the accompanying actions and activities became as important as the final result, since they allowed for the community to come together, reminisce, and talk about their loss.

> By cementing stones on roofs, I became a link between generations, between loss and love, between together and alone, between practical and spiritual, between life and death ... It feels good because I feel part of a tradition. It feels humble because I didn't invent it. I feel elementary because I can be close to my dead father and my dead son.[16]

Valentine and Barbara also created a ritual for the loss of the embrace together, *Omarme*, which seems particular relevant for the present Covid-crisis, with its measures of social distancing.

The Cypriot choreographer Lia Haraki created the dance theater piece *Monday Mourning* in 2006, after the unexpected death of her father. The work is

> a comment on mourning and the different ways it is being expressed. ... With the death, abandonment or separation of a loved one, reality as we know it changes and that is why we mourn. The time we take to mourn is the transitional period before we get used to our new reality.[17]

With *Monday Mourning*, Lia pays tribute to her father's joyful attitude toward life, exemplified by his fondness of popular music and dancing. The piece brings five characters onto the stage, all of whom are dealing with their mourning in different ways. Michael,

an actor in a business suit, wanders around the stage carrying a briefcase, suspended in a state of aimless, lethargic waiting. At one point, he explodes into a theatrical solo in which he uses a variety of props to attempt suicide: shooting himself with a gun, drinking poison, trying to hang himself with his tie, or electrocuting himself with a string of Christmas lights, all set to the Elvis song *I want you, I need you, I love you*. Evie, a dancer, embodies a grieving older woman who quietly goes about completing all the necessary rites and rituals of death: using dead branches, colorful string, incense, and prayers, she turns the stage into a graveyard. Her actions are accompanied by a traditional *moirolói*. Cathryn, a singer, vocally accompanies the others, but also tells her own stories of loss and separation. Her stories illustrate the five stages of grief, from denial to acceptance.

> I wish I could walk down the street holding your arm again
> I wish we could have one of our big, ugly arguments
> once more
> I wish I could hold you and tell you I am sorry
> I wish I could read your eyes again
> I wish you would read me one of your awful poems again
> I wish I could ask you more questions
> I wish I could leave you too.[18]

Lia herself dances a series of duets with a twin or doppelgänger: two girls who, faced with loss, continue to embrace life. Together, they perform a series of comical dance acts set to some of her father's favorite musical theater songs. *Monday Mourning* ends with all the characters coming together to the song *Somewhere over the Rainbow* from *The Wizard of Oz*, toasting each other, embracing, and eventually dancing together in a shared ritual.

In her book *Au bonheur des morts: Récits de ceux qui restent* (For the happiness of the dead. Stories of those who remain, 2015, 2017), the Belgian philosopher Vinciane Despret argues that dialogues with the dead are necessary not only because they support 'those who remain' in their mourning processes, but also because they offer the deceased a prolongation of their lives. This 'second life' is clearly a very different proposition than their first life, but it is nevertheless more than just a metaphorical idea. Despret's book is full of examples of laments or other forms of dialogue that give a voice to the dead and can lead to concrete actions that influence the present for the better. One of the examples that Despret gives is of the French comedian Patrick Chesnais, whose son died in an accident. After his son's death, Chesnais continued to leave him messages on his answerphone and later started writing him letters. For Chesnais, this continuing dialogue helps 'to keep his son alive, in another way.' Despret in turn concludes that these kinds of dialogues with the dead 'not only allow the dead to exist, but also give them permission to change the life of those to whom they respond.'[19] Similarly, the Belgian artistic project *Post office 00/00/00*[20] actively initiates a dialogue with the dead. People are invited to send letters to deceased loved ones. One of the visual artists involved in the project, who is part of the 'post office,' responds to the letters with a drawing.

Most *moirológhia* include a section in which the dead are called by their name, often in a kind of recurring refrain. The ancient Greek verb *anakalema* describes this practice, which literally means 'to call upon' or 'to invoke.' It is used in the ancient ritual of calling the dead by name at their tomb, in order to raise their spirit from the grave and ask for their help or for a favor.[21] It is also used in Aeschylus's play *The Persians* to invoke the spirit of the dead king Darius (see also next chapter). In contemporary Cyprus, both the word and the practice are still in popular usage.[22]

Telling stories about the deceased fulfils a similar function. Stories do more than just help us to remember:

> They also make things happen. They create. They are sensitive and touch you. They bring things and worlds into existence, they metamorphose. They are first and foremost experiences. ... The stories keep the presence present, the dead alive. ... They are performances![23]

One story of a death in the past that interacts strongly with the present is told in *zero degrees* (2005), the iconic artistic exchange between Sidi Larbi Cherkaoui and Akram Khan that I accompanied as a dramaturg. As the piece begins, Akram narrates an incident that happened in his life. A second-generation immigrant to the UK, he traveled to his ancestors' countries, India and Bangladesh, to confront questions about his in-between identity. 'And what I remember is...' Akram's story starts with the crossing of a border. He is asked to prove his identity, an identity that in this moment completely coincides with a document: his passport.

> Suddenly I realized how vulnerable I felt because if that
> passport disappears where is my proof of identity? They
> could just say I am Bangladeshi. I am a bandit. It is amazing
> how much power a passport holds. A passport holds
> between a good life and a bad life, between life and death.
> I mean, it holds everything in just a piece of paper.[24]

As his journey unfolds, Akram discovers that he is a foreigner in
his country of origin. He self-mockingly describes himself:

> It is really hot, and I just feel like, I just need to get to a
> hotel. Initially we were gonna go to live with some friends.
> But I thought: no, I need my conveniences. I need my
> essential supplies. And those were: a bathroom, a bath, a
> hot shower, television, MTV. The usual things that we are
> used to in the West.

A foreigner who needs his cousin to explain the local customs
to him and prevent him from getting into trouble because of his
ignorance and his different ways of behaving: 'It is not my clothing,
I don't think. It is just my mannerisms. They can identify that I am
a foreigner. And maybe it is arrogance.'[25]

Akram's narrative forms the backbone of *zero degrees*. It is
made up of four parts, which are spread across the entire length of
the piece. They are interspersed with several movement sections,
all of which are based on simple ideas that were developed in movement research sessions by Akram and Larbi, jointly or separately.
The dance sequences organically find a connection with parts of
Akram's narrative. The specific hand movements that accompany
the first part of the narrative, for example, are further explored in
a later movement sequence for hands and arms, in which the two
dancers explore how their identities mirror each other. Their duet
is followed by a second one, which explores the turns (or *paltas*) of
the Indian classical dance form *kathak* in a contemporary way and
leads to a fight sequence and a first separation, allowing Akram
to manipulate Larbi's body like a basketball. This then leads into
Larbi's solo in which his dummy abuses him.

The 'dummies,' as the artistic team fondly nicknamed
them, are life-sized replicas of Akram and Larbi's bodies. They
were contributed to the production by the British visual artist and
Turner Prize winner Antony Gormley, for whom *zero degrees* was

the first stage design. Best known for positioning copper casts of his own body in urban and rural environments such as the City of London, Crosby Beach in Liverpool, and the Swiss Alps, he created plaster casts of Akram and Larbi to heighten the 'twin' motif of resemblance. But they also function as puppets, which enables the dancers to treat their doubled bodies in an uncanny, violent way that wouldn't have been possible with real bodies. Kenneth Gross, in his book *Puppet: An Essay on Uncanny Life* (2011), writes that this is one of the puppet's main functions. The puppeteer Sue Buckmaster[26] writes in her MA thesis 'A Psychoanalytical Study of the Power of the Puppet' (1997) that 'puppets have a subversive power to act out what we normally feel should be repressed behavior.' She goes on to say that 'their most subversive act is their ability to make us confront our acknowledgment of death.'[27] In the last days of the rehearsal process for *zero degrees*, we developed a number of short scenes with the dummies that would become interludes, some of them quite subversive but also offering comic relief. An example is a scene in which Larbi kicks Akram's dummy, while the real Akram acts out the impact it receives.

All the movement sections eventually connect with the main narrative. Shaolin-inspired moves, which originate in Akram's and Larbi's shared admiration for Bruce Lee, physicalize Akram's verbal fight with the border guards. The percussive footwork of kathak illustrates the relentlessness of the train journey. Two thirds into the narrative, the story shifts from its original question of identity to a story about a dead body on a train.

> So I am looking at this person
> And I am going, he is playing tricks on me
> But then, something dawns upon me
> And I go to my cousin: is this person moving?
> He is just lying on the floor
> He has just got a torn T-shirt, a longi, which is a very
> long skirt
> And he is going; no he is dead
> And I am going: fuck this man is dead
> I have never seen a dead body
> We have got to do something
> We have got to tell the police
> Suddenly you hear this screaming lady

> And she is going: please, my husband has just died
> Will somebody help me take him off the train?
> And you know when somebody cries
> And it is genuine, you feel emotion conjure up on you[28]

From this point in the narrative onward, *zero degrees* becomes a contemporary lament for the dead body on the train, performed in different languages and traditions. Akram tells the story once more without words, using *abhinaya*, the storytelling element of kathak. Larbi re-enacts it as a comical farce, using the dummies as puppets. Akram then dances a contemporary solo around his dummy, becoming the aura around his own dead body. Finally, Larbi sings a lament, holding his dummy in a pietà-like manner.

The song that Larbi sings at the end of *zero degrees* is *Yerushalayim shel Zagar* (Jerusalem the Golden), the semi-official anthem of the State of Israel, which was originally sung by Naomi Shemer. It tells the story of a people in exile who eventually return home to their city. Larbi's choice of this song is inspired by a complex web of motives. By using a Yiddish song, he, an 'Arab,' reaches out to the Other.

> We thought it would be interesting to use the voice of the other culture that is supposed to be our opposite in order to express a shared desire: to return home. To say it with the words of the one that is a stranger to us.[29]

But the song also confirms his belief in the interrelatedness of all cultures and traditions, especially as he had discovered that the melody goes back to a Basque lullaby. Larbi sings the original song in a lamenting manner, mixing his voice with Sufi singer Faheem Mazhar.

Underneath the performance text of Larbi's lament for the anonymous body in Akram's story is a subtext in which Larbi reaches out to and mourns his own dead father. When Larbi was nineteen, shortly after his parents had divorced and his father had returned to Morocco, his father died unexpectedly. Because the divorce had been caused in part by his father's inability to understand and support his son—accepting neither his homosexuality nor his talent as a dancer—Larbi's grief became more complex and laden with guilt, in addition to the more usual emotions of sadness and anger. Part of his anger was directed at himself.

Early on in his career, Larbi danced in Alain Platel's piece *Iets op Bach* (1998). At the time, Platel asked all the dancers to create a solo that 'is better than anything you have created or seen before.' Larbi's solo, set to Bach's cantata BWV 82, *Ich habe genug*, ends with him violently setting himself on fire. Self-inflicted violence would remain an important motif in many of his early works: he crashed into walls in his first full-length work *Rien de rien* (2000) and was beaten up by a puppet, his mirror image, in both *zero degrees* (2005) and *Apocrifu* (2007). In her essay on Larbi's work, 'Gezocht: zelf' (Seeking the Self, 2008), the Indian poet Karthika Naïr describes how 'death abounds in almost all of Mr. Cherkaoui's work: either as loss, or—often—as self-destruction in one form or the other.'[30] Naïr quotes Larbi as stating that death strengthens the link with our ancestors and that this is a condition for personal growth and regeneration.

In 2004, Larbi was invited to create a contemporary ballet for Les Ballets de Monte-Carlo, his first commission for the company. *In Memoriam* (2004) was created shortly after the death of his mother's new partner. Larbi's presence at the funeral reminded him that he had been absent from his father's funeral, but being part of this event also meant that he could begin to relive his older, partially un-lived mourning. The ballet explores and expresses our links with our ancestors: how they continue to survive in us. 'As a child, my facial expression resembled a lot my mother's. After the death of my father, it changed. I started to look like him. Part of me reincarnated my father.'[31] *In Memoriam* is the first part of a trilogy that Larbi created for Les Ballets de Monte-Carlo, in which he explored the theme of death, creating meaningful links between his own personal experiences and larger, historical, and contemporary traumas. *Mea Culpa* (2006), the second piece in the trilogy, addresses the collective Western guilt of the colonial and post-colonial exploitation of a large part of the world. Having looked at the past of our ancestors and the present of post-colonial inequalities, *Memento Mori* (2017), the third part of the trilogy on death, asks what kind of future Larbi wishes he could leave for the generations to come. Instead of the weight of individual or collective traumas and the accumulated waste of environmental exploitation, his wish is to leave as few traces as possible. Both visually and musically, the atmosphere of the piece is futuristic. The stage design is a circular light grid that moves up and down like a UFO, and the score by musician Woodkid includes voice recordings sent into space by NASA. One of the central movement patterns is the spiral, with the dancers spiraling around their own axis and into the emptiness of space, appearing and disappearing like ghosts.

The concept of synchronicity as it was first introduced by Carl Gustav Jung suggests that people with artistic sensibilities are often able to tune into the unforeseen and unpredictable realities of the world, without necessarily being aware of what is about to happen. *zero degrees* was due to premiere in London on July 12, 2005, when the 7/7 suicide bomb attacks took place on the London Underground. As a result, both the performers and their audiences experienced the first performances of *zero degrees* as a lament for the victims of the attacks—who were all, in fact, 'dead bodies on trains.' The emotional charge and release of these first performances remained strong throughout the production's touring life, which lasted until the final performance in New York in the spring of 2008.

As I mentioned in the introduction to this book, it was the Covid-19 lockdown that gave me the time to finish writing it. Early on in the lockdown I also heard about the exhibition *Trauern: Von Verlust und Veränderung* (*Mourning On Loss and Change*), which had been curated by Brigitte Kölle at the Hamburger Kunsthalle. In the introduction to the exhibition catalogue, Kölle writes:

> We all have to grapple at some point in our lives with anguishing experiences of disappointment, failure and irreversible change. Whether it is the loss of a loved one through separation or death, departing from cherished ideals and visions, or being deprived of one's home and familiar surroundings—every human being knows what it means to lose someone or something. Although these experiences of loss affect each of us differently, the way we deal, describe and assess them also depends on our cultural, social and political environment. Mourning is politically significant and allows conclusions to be drawn about social conditions and inadequacies.[32]

My first trip after travel restrictions were lifted was to Hamburg to see this exhibition. It was as much a personal pilgrimage as a professional engagement. The exhibition brought together works by contemporary and twentieth-century artists who have explored the notion of grief and mourning in different media: painting, sculpture, photography, video, and graphic art. The journey through the exhibition spaces was beautifully curated around several themes, including 'Melancholy and Mourning,' 'Grief and Gender,' 'Collective Mourning,' and 'Mourning and Protest.'

Watching the short black-and-white silent film *I'm too sad to tell you* (1970–1971) by the Dutch artist Bas Jan Ader, I can already distantly hear the soundtrack of another art work in the next room. Brigitte Kölle later tells me that this is an unintentional side-effect of the Covid-19 crisis, due to extra security measures such as allowing fewer visitors in certain rooms and removing soundproof curtains to improve air circulation. For me, this accident reveals something special. As I am watching the detailed facial choreography of Ader weeping in front of the camera, I hear melancholic singing in the distance. The effect is almost one of synesthesia, a connection between two different senses and experiences. The movements of Ader's eyes and mouth, his breathing and swallowing, his occasional hand gestures, suggest a tension between trying to stay in control of his emotions and surrendering to them. The unexpected soundtrack comes from another video: *God* (2007) by the Icelandic artist Ragnar Kjartansson. It shows Kjartansson as a Sinatra-esque singer in a black tuxedo repeating a single line over and over, accompanied by a ballroom orchestra: for more than thirty minutes, he sings nothing but 'Sorrow conquers happiness.' The repetitive nature of the work captures the relentlessness of any mourning process. Kjartansson's video touches me and also makes me smile. Like many of the other works in the exhibition, it shows that a certain 'artificiality' and sometimes even a sense of ironic distance can be helpful in allowing us to relive our mourning. In 2013, Kjartansson made a similar video for a MoMA PS1 event, when he asked the rock band The National to play their three-and-half-minute song *Sorrow*, live on stage, continuously for six hours, more than a hundred times. The video *A Lot of Sorrow* (2014) captures the event and how the song transforms over time and becomes 'sculptural.'

As I continue walking through the exhibition, I am excited to discover an explicit reference to another living tradition of laments, just across the border from Zagori, in Albania. *Vajtocja* (2002), one of several videos by the Albanian film and performance artist Adrian Paci, starts with the artist knocking on the door of a house in a rural village and being received by an elderly woman. While he puts on his best suit, she prepares a bed for him in the next room. He then lies down on it so that she can start singing her lament for him. She covers her head with a scarf before she starts her weeping song, which she accompanies with simple but meaningful hand gestures, while her upper body sways back and forth as if in a state of trance. Eventually, she starts touching and caressing the body, before ending her lament abruptly with a stylized cry: 'ooi ooi ay.' Paci then gets up from the bed and thanks her matter-of-factly. The lightness of the ending, which again makes me smile, reminds me of my own experiences in Greece, where the lamenters would bring their audience to tears, only to switch to telling jokes and laughing heartily moments later.

Visiting this exhibition also reminded me of another exhibition that I saw almost a decade ago at the Vancouver Art Gallery in Canada: the installation *Waste Not* by the Chinese artist Song Dong, which he had created in collaboration with his mother, Zhao Xiangyuan. *Waste Not* or *Wu Jin Qi Yong* refers to the Chinese virtue of frugality, which Song's mother abided by all her life, never throwing anything away. In an attempt to counteract the scarcity and poverty that she and her family had grown up in, she kept everything, accumulating tens of thousands of worn, broken and occasionally unused objects: old toys and dolls, piles of second-hand clothes and unused fabric, empty bottles, plastic fast-food containers, shopping bags, containers full of medicines long past their expiration dates, and even fossilized remnants of soap bars. Her hoarding became even more obsessive after her husband's death.

In their book *Death, Memory and Material Culture* (2001), Elizabeth Hallam and Jenny Hockney offer many historical and contemporary examples of 'how the dead and the living find proximity via material objects and places.'[33] They describe how the 'recovery of discarded objects and the reinterpretation of those things that are overlooked, devalued or remain "invisible" from dominant social, economic or political perspective, has been an important strategy in artistic discourses.'[34]

This orientation toward used material fragments still resonates when translated into the personal worlds of those facing loss through the death of loved ones: the entire contents of a house shaken by a recent death, from old shopping lists to worn shoes, may speak to years of accumulated memories.[35]

In her memoir, Song's mother uses a very similar phrase when she explains her attachment to all her accumulated objects: 'All these many items are not merely specimens, rather they are lives that were lived. ... The reason I've tried, by every means possible, to hold on to those things, is so as to extend their lives.'[36]

With his project, Song invited his mother to remove all her objects from her house and place them in an exhibition context instead. His primary motive was to encourage her to let go of things by giving them another use, in order for 'her pathological attachment to the past' to be cured. He says that he wanted to pull her 'out of her isolated world filled with grief.'[37] Part of the skeletal wooden frame of her house became the central piece of the exhibition, with all her objects arranged around it, organized by material and function.

For me, seeing the installation was extremely moving. By the time I saw it in Canada it had already been touring around the world for several years, and the catalogue referenced some of the reactions of its earlier audiences. In South Korea, Germany, the UK, and the USA 'it evoked strong responses from the audience, some of whom wept in front of it as if encountering a long-lost friend or relative.'[38] I had a similar reaction, as it triggered my own memories and experiences. After my father died, I became an obsessive collector, starting with the model cars that he had given me as a present. Later I expanded my collections to encompass shells, stamps, and card decks. Whatever act of collecting I embarked upon, it was done with an obsession and rigor that is not typical for how an average child deals with the objects it collects. The exhibition also brought up memories of my grandmother, who was born in the aftermath of World War I and was a young mother during World War II. In order to be prepared for any new crisis situation, she kept a huge stock of all kinds of supplies, including bars of green soap similar to those that Song's mother had collected.

Unpacking and arranging the objects was a performative part of the installation that allowed Song's mother to reminisce about and share the stories associated with the objects, both with her children and with the first audiences. Some of these stories were published in the exhibition catalogue and became an integral part of the project. Outside the gallery, a sentence in neon lights would light up the building. The text was part of a direct dialogue between Song and his dead father: 'Dad, don't worry! Mum and us are fine.'

When I saw the exhibition in Vancouver, Song's mother was no longer alive. She died unexpectedly in an accident in 2009. Song continued to assemble the exhibition with the support of his sister. Now it was their turn to prolong their mother's life through the objects she had collected. They convinced themselves 'that her spirit was actually there, among the things she gathered around herself for so many years.'[39]

As I was working on this book project, a desire grew in me to create my own lament for my dead father, which could also be a lament for any victim of a traffic accident. At the time I was engaging with the practice of 'dream opening,' which was developed by the American psychologist Catherine Shainberg[40] in her School of Images (SOI) and is based on an ancient Sephardic kabbalah tradition. The practice teaches you to better remember your dreams in order to 'open' them, that is, to look at their meaningful patterns and eventually become a conscious dreamer. While I was doing this work with Claudia Zackariya, one of Shainberg's students, I twice dreamt about the solo I wanted to create and I was able to imagine its three-part structure.

My *Skeleton Dance* begins with me transforming into my younger self—the child I was before and after my father's accident. One of the few memories I have of my father are the matchbox toy cars that he would always bring me as a present. When I found out that my younger brother had kept many of them for his own children to play with, I was able to reclaim them and play with them myself. The child organizes the cars in rows, drives them around the table, under it and off the tabletop, eventually enacting tiny car crashes.

In the second part of the solo, this innocent child's play begins to affect the entire body of the adult me. It becomes a wild dance, set to different versions of Nancy Sinatra's farewell song *Bang Bang*. I express both anger and self-inflicted pain. Eventually the energy quietens down again and transitions into the third part of the solo, during which I sing my self-composed lament. I have developed several written versions of it, but I also want to continue to improvise parts of it so that I can tune in to particularly meaningful moments and places. Here is just one possible version:

Dad,
You left me your golden watch
The one you were wearing

When you crashed, crashed
I wore it myself
Although it was broken
Tik Tok Tik Tok Tik Tok
You tied me
Please unknot me
Xi oh Xi
I am sorry my death scared you
Xi oh Xi
I am sorry my death scarred you
Xi oh Xi
I am sorry I haunted you
Xi oh Xi
I am sorry I kept you embraced
I untie you, my son

In his essay 'Downscaling Lamentation: On Trope and Fratricide' (2014), Nimrod Reitman writes that the lament

> ...is never restricted to one creed, or even to the parameters of language, for it feeds on the frenzy of nonlinguistic try-outs such as the sigh, the sob, the ululation, the desperate murmur, the thud, the cry and other corporeal sonorities that have no proper container in language and music.[41]

As a result, organized religions have tried to contain, to restrain, and 'to tame this plaintive havoc' with a range of other musical genres. 'A whole canon of operas, cantatas, vespers, madrigals, and responsorial music depend on and have originated with some form of lamentation.'[42] The Catholic Requiem Mass is a particular case in point, in which an entire musical Mass is dedicated to the memory of the deceased. A Requiem is not a lament. For that its musical structure is too complex and too composed but it has a similar function, that is to bring together the community within the context of a mass to honor the death.

At the same time that Sidi Larbi Cherkaoui created *Memento Mori* for Les Ballets de Monte-Carlo, he also created *Requiem* (2017) for the Ballet Flanders. He chose Gabriel Fauré's version of the requiem mass, in a rearrangement by the Antwerp composer Wim Henderickx, who also added new parts to it: a prologue, an epilogue and a new central section entitled *Lament*. The lament is an aria for the French-Algerian soprano Amel Brahim-Djelloul, which became the new musical and emotional heart of the work. The new orchestration combined the luminosity and hopefulness of the original with a certain gravitas, reflecting on what was happening in the world at the time. It commemorated the victims of several terrorist attacks as well as the many refugees drowning in the Mediterranean. As in the ancient Greek tragedies (see also next chapter), the chorus, which consisted of both the adult and children's choruses of the Opera Flanders, plays a central role in Larbi's *Requiem*. Dressed in funeral clothes belonging to different traditions, they perform the universal hand and arm gestures of prayer: holding the palms together, putting them on the floor or on their hearts, or stretching them out in front of them to touch the transparent walls, which are built out of window frames. The chorus is there to support the individual performers, who are dancing mainly in couples, each made up of a man and a woman. The voices of the soprano and the baritone are mirrored by a series of danced duets, which demonstrate how female and male energies can carry and support each other's grief in different ways. *Requiem* is a danced prayer that is passed on from one duet to the next. In the process, it transforms, becoming softer and more and more fluent, as if layers of grief are being peeled off. 'I really believe that to heal from a trauma or grief, you need a physical act. You have to move. Mourning is dancing. I think we have to dance to mourn.'[43]

In January 2018, two artists I admire a lot and whose artistic dialogue I was able to witness from a privileged position, the composer Fabrizio Cassol and the choreographer Alain Platel, premiered their work *Requiem pour L.* in Berlin. The production was a continuation of previous artistic creations in which they had collaborated on contemporary interpretations of iconic pieces of music from the classical canon: *VSPRS* (2006) referenced the *Maria Vespers* by Claudio Monteverdi and *pitié* (2008) was a version of Johann Sebastian Bach's *St Matthew Passion*. With *Requiem pour L.*, Fabrizio had wanted to adapt Mozart's legendary unfinished *Requiem* in a similar way, continuing his collaboration with the Congolese and South-African musicians he had worked with before. The piece was also a kind of sequel to an earlier piece, *Coup Fatal* (2014), in which music from the Western Baroque repertoire had been performed with African music and rhythms. Fabrizio writes about *Requiem pour L.*:

<blockquote>

Already at the exploratory stage, there were some fundamental questions: how might some sections be replaced by
influences from elsewhere? And how to reframe the ritual
of the *Requiem*, so imbued with sadness, in order to incor-
porate other emotions, such as joy, transcended by music
and dancing?[44]

</blockquote>

Early on in the conceptual preparation of the work, Alain had the idea of juxtaposing the musical universe of the piece with 'a literal representation of death.' He was inspired by Sophie Calie, who had filmed her dying mother for *Pas pu saisir la mort* (I couldn't capture death, 2007), and by Bill Viola, who had paired images of the birth of his son with images of his dying mother in his *Nantes Triptych* (1992).

<blockquote>

For *Requiem*, I am searching an image that represents death
as literally as possible and that shows how infinitely small
the moment of dying is, just a sigh ... I have this idea to
project during the whole performance the close-up of the
face of a dying person. ... A face which still reveals the small
signs of life, until you no longer see them once death has
taken place.[45]

</blockquote>

When the performance starts, I see nothing but an empty stage set made up of differently-sized black cubes, which clearly refer-ences the Holocaust *Denkmal*, or *Memorial to the Murdered Jews of Europe*, in Berlin. The background is a large black-and-white projection of the face of a woman lying on pillows with a flower motif, her eyes closed. She is lying there very peacefully, occasion-ally opening her eyes, wetting her lips with her tongue, or touching her face. The image of her face is only occasionally blurred when another person passes in front of the camera, unrecognized. Five musicians, enter the stage one by one, followed by six singers, all of whom touch the black cubes or pick up one of the small stones that are scattered across them.

During the piece's creation process, Alain had contacted a long-time friend, the physician Marc Cosyns, who had been involved in the campaign to legalize euthanasia in Belgium, to ask him if he could help him find a patient who would allow herself to be filmed while she was dying. By some meaningful coincidence of life, another friend they had in common—L (for Lucie)—requested

euthanasia around the same time. L. had been an outspoken feminist and political activist who had contributed significantly to the legalization of both abortion and euthanasia. L. gave her permission for Alain to film her death.

In every creative process there is a certain amount of distance between an original idea and the final result or art work, but in this particular case the subject was so sensitive that every choice and every decision needed to be examined very closely, not only on artistic but also on ethical grounds. Alain kept a diary throughout the process, which was eventually published. It gives a detailed account of the piece's creative journey, from its inception to its reception, and all the doubts that Alain had along the way. It also references many of his previous encounters with death: the loss of an old classmate, his father, his first dog, and his close friend, the opera director Gerard Mortier.

Musically, *Requiem pour L.* begins with an accordion solo. The other instruments and singers gradually join in as the music touches on various genres, from opera to gospel. At one point there is a long silence during which the musicians appear frozen, allowing the viewers to focus on the intimate encounter with L.'s face. L. opens her eyes. Occasionally her eyes widen, staying open a little longer. She smiles. Sometimes another person's hand appears in the camera frame to gently touch or caress her.

Alain's diary shows that he is seriously considering and at times questioning the ethical implications of his artistic choice to use the video of L.'s death. These considerations are present at every stage of the creative process. Early on, it is decided that only one static camera will be in the room, and that it will be operated by one of the family members who has volunteered to start and stop it. It is agreed that L.'s family (her husband and children) own the images. They decide if and when they are ready and willing to release them. If at any stage in the creative process they feel uncomfortable, they can withdraw their permission for the images to be used. Alain also considers the impact of the images on the creative team. Whenever he himself watches the video or shows it to his artistic collaborators, he checks in with them afterwards. On showing them to the filmmaker Simon Van Rompay, who edits the video for the stage, he is reassured by Simon's assertion that the images resonate 'peace and serenity,' and that it is 'as if you have been given permission to watch them.'[46] The showing of the video at different stages of the creative process becomes a ritual in itself, allowing the family and all those involved in the production to experience an emotional release.

Achieving the right balance between live performance and screen projection in any contemporary stage production is difficult, but in this piece the challenge is even greater. Fabrizio Cassol is adamant that his music cannot be reduced to sounding like the soundtrack to a film. In the editing process of the film, Alain Platel is alert to the danger of adding too many filmic effects (such as slow-motion or close-ups) that could affect the authenticity of the experience, giving the impression of it being staged for particular effects. In the end, a few simple artistic decisions are sufficient: the video is presented in black-and-white, and the focus remains solely on L., with no other people appearing on the screen. During the rehearsal process, the relationship between the live performance and the video is the subject of extensive research, enabling the performers to subtly direct the audience's focus with their timing:

> On specific scenes we work in detail. When the *Libera* is sung, we empty the stage and we see in the film how Marc asks L. if she stays with her decision. You see her nod yes, with a smile. The last time L. opens her eyes, she is accompanied by a heart-breaking solo by Niels on the tuba. He seems to cry, to scream, to wail, to weep and to sigh, all at the same time. The moment L. dies happens during the Samoa dance on stage, which takes all the attention. When it becomes silent and you notice again the film images, you realize you have missed the actual moment of death.[47]

The music evolves in energetic waves, often starting with an instrumental solo that grows in texture and volume and eventually returns to a meaningful silence. In the *Dies irae primum*, Fredy Massamba steps onto one of the black cubes. Holding a white handkerchief in his hands, he directly addresses the others and L. on the screen and performs, in his native language of Kilari, what most resembles a traditional lament.

> I am going away on a long journey to meet my kindred
> Crossing rivers and oceans.
> Leaving behind me a whole people searching for hope.
> I am going a long way, but my spirit will remain here.

You are the tiny streams that will become great rivers.
My melancholy journey is eternal rest.
I thank you for having shared with me the most difficult and most precious moments.
Tell my children to keep my loincloths and my jewelry, to pass them on their own offspring.
Tears of grief overcome me.
After fighting so many battles, I must leave now.
It is all accomplished! Embrace life to the full.[48]

Eventually, all the singers jump onto the gravestones and the music builds to a climax that ends abruptly in another silence. L. closes her eyes. As the wailing tuba solo starts, the singers shake their colorful necklaces and beat their chests. Just as Alain resisted using any editing effects in the video, he keeps his choreography very simple. The subtle movements and small ritual gestures resonate with something the French psychiatrist Fernand Deligny[49] has said: 'Every small gesture speaks.' The lighting design and the larger group movements on stage, too, are organized in such a way as to keep the right balance between music and image. There are only two choreographed dance sections for the entire group: the first is the Samoa dance, which consists of fast and complex hand and arm movements and is set to the *Sanctus*, and the second one is the finale, which is inspired by South-African gumboot dances.

The final part of Alain's diary gives an overview of the reception of the work. The team have discussions among themselves and with the presenters on how best to frame the performance. A few days after the premiere, the father of a good friend decides to die consciously. The premiere is dedicated to all the deaths that occurred during the creation process. Each performance becomes a re-enactment of the wake at L.'s deathbed, honoring her death, but also her life.

Everyone brings his own death to *Requiem pour L.*[50]

# Notes


1   Phelan 1997, p. 3.
2   Wilce 2009, p. 1.
3   Rilke, from *Requiem*, in Mitchell
    1982-1989, p. 82 (Michell's
    translation, p. 83):
        Ob man nicht dennoch hätte
        Klagefrauen
        Auftreiben müssen? Weiber,
        welche weinen
        Für Geld, und die man so
        bezahlen kann,
        daß sie die Nacht durch heulen,
        wenn es still wird.
        Gebräuche her! wir haben nicht
        genug
        Gebräuche. Alles geht und wird
        verredet.
        So mußt du kommen, tot, und
        hier mit mir
        Klagen nachholen. Hörst du,
        daß ich Klage?
4   From a personal email, March 2nd,
    2002.
5   From Snelling's unpublished
    Notebook, *anendingbeginning*.
6   Butler 2004, p. 22.
7   From a personal email from Lin
    Snelling, May 22nd, 2020.
8   From the performance text of *EVA*.
9   Raes 2017, p. 9.
10  www.beyondthespoken.eu.
11  HAU 2017, p. 7.
12  Ibid., p. 11.
13  Ibid., p. 91.
14  Ibid., pp. 20-21.
15  The area close to the French border
    and the North-Sea, also reputed for its
    Flanders Fields of World War I.
16  Kempynck's unpublished presentation
    notes of the symposium *Open Einde*
    (*Open End*) in Ghent, October 16th,
    2016.
17  From the press dossier of
    *Monday Mourning*.
18  From the performance text of
    *Monday Mourning*.
19  Despret 2015, p. 15: 'Répondre
    accomplit non seulement l'existence
    du mort, mais l'autorise à modifier la
    vie de ceux qui répondent.'
20  See: postkantoor.org.
21  See also Alexiou 2002, pp. 109-110.
22  It was my friend Alexis Vassiliou,
    the director of the Dance House
    Lemesos, who drew my attention
    to this.
23  Despret 2015, 2017, pp. 204-205: 'Les
    histoires font, et elles font que quelque
    chose se passe. Elles créent. Elles sont
    sensibles et elles touchent. Elles font
    exister des choses et des mondes, elles
    métamorphosent, mais surtout, elles
    sont des expériences. ... Les histoires
    gardent la présence présente, le mort
    vivant. ... Ce sont des performances.'
24  From the performance text of
    *zero degrees*.
25  Ibid.
26  See also Cools 2016, pp. 179-197.
27  Buckmaster 1997, p. 27.
28  From the performance text of *zero
    degrees*.
29  Cherkaoui 2006, p. 53: 'Nous
    trouvions intéressant de passer de
    l'autre côté, d'utiliser la voix de la
    culture qui nous est prétendument
    opposée, pour exprimer un même
    désir: l'envie de rentrer chez soi.'
30  Naïr 2008, p. 116.
31  Cherkaoui 2006, p. 54: 'Enfant, mon
    visage ressemblait beaucoup à celui de
    ma mère. Après la mort de mon père,
    il s'est transformé. J'ai commencé
    à lui ressembler. Une partie de moi
    réincarnait mon père.'
32  Kölle 2020.
33  Hallam 2001, p. 6.
34  Ibid., p. 12.
35  Ibid., p. 12.
36  Wu 2009, p. 13.
37  Ibid., p. 19.
38  Ibid., p. 2.
39  Ibid., p. 60.
40  See Shainberg 2005.
41  Reitman 2014, pp. 248-249.
42  Ibid., p. 249.
43  Cherkaoui in the program text of
    *Requiem*, Ballet Flanders, p. 45.
44  From the booklet accompanying the
    CD release of *Requiem pour L.*, p. 8.
45  Platel 2019, p. 115: 'Want voor
    *Requiem* zoek ik namelijk een beeld
    dat die dood zo letterlijk mogelijk
    toont en dat laat zien hoe dat moment
    zo ontzettend klein is, een zucht ook.
    ... Vandaar mijn idee om gedurende de
    hele voorstelling een close-up van een
    gelaat van een stervende te laten zien.
    ... Alleen een close-up van het gezicht
    waarop je eerst nog kleine tekenen
    van leven ziet, die je dan misschien
    niet echt meer ontwaart wanneer dat
    moment van sterven echt plaatsvindt.'
46  Ibid. p. 142: 'Het gevoel ook dat je
    naar de beelden "mag kijken."'
47  Ibid. p. 215: 'Op bepaalde scènes
    werken we heel specifiek. Wanneer
    het *Libera* wordt gezongen, maken
    we het plateau leeg en zien we in de
    film hoe Marc aan L. vraagt of ze nog

altijd bij haar beslissing blijft. Je ziet haar breed glimlachend ja knikken. De laatste keren dat L. haar ogen opent, worden begeleid door een hartverscheurende solo van Niels op de tuba: hij lijkt te schreien, schreeuwen, loeien, huilen en zuchten tegelijk. Het moment waarop L. effectief sterft, verloopt terwijl op de scène de Samoa-dans plaatsvindt. Die trekt alle aandacht naar zich toe en als het daarna stil wordt en je de filmbeelden weer opmerkt, besef je dat je het eigenlijke doodgaan hebt gemist.'

48 From the CD, *Requiem pour L.*, p. 17.
49 Deligny has been one of Platel's main sources of inspiration throughout his entire career.
50 Platel 2019, p. 261: 'Naar *Requiem pour L.* brengt elkeen zijn eigen doden mee.'

# Laments as a Collective Form of Witnessing

I       'We are here to witness. There is nothing else to do.'[1]

By referencing Peter Eisenman's Holocaust *Denkmal* in Berlin in his set design for *Requiem pour L.*, Alain Platel deliberately links L.'s individual death to a much larger, historically charged mourning process. It is a strategy that other artists have used, too. In the second chapter, for example, we saw how Philippe Forest links his mourning for the death of his daughter to the collective mourning for the victims of Nagasaki in his novel *Sarinagara* (2004).

The Norwegian choreographer Per Roar Thorsnes successfully completed a practice-based PhD at the University of the Arts in Helsinki on the subject of 'Griefscapes—choreographic strategies for embodying traumatic contexts' (2015). Thorsnes defines griefscapes as 'the affective and entangled—though often ephemeral and invisible—impact that traumatic contexts of grieving can have in circumscribing our lives by being present through what is absent.'[2] As part of his artistic research he created a trilogy of performances, collectively entitled *Life and Death*, between 2003 and 2006, in which he gradually moved from the personal to the communal. The first piece in the trilogy, *A Song to Martin* (2003), deals with his personal grief for his friend, Martin Hoftun, who died in an airplane crash. Subtitled 'a study in the anatomy of grieving,' Thorsnes writes about it: 'The aim was to translate my private grieving and give it a body in the choreographed performance that could have a public interest and relevance.'[3] In the final piece, *An Unfinished Story* (2006), Thorsnes deals with collective forms of mourning in the aftermath of the Bosnian war (1992–1995) and the Srebrenica genocide, parts of which he witnessed, having visited refugee camps and the city of Mostar as early as 1994. Subtitled 'a study in the neurology of loss,' it focuses on 'the bodily states of the psychosomatic reaction patterns that tended to occur when coping with post-traumatic stress.'[4] *An Unfinished Story* premiered at the Vijećnica, Sarajevo's former City Hall and national library, and involved performers from Oslo, Belgrade, and Sarajevo. Just as Alain Platel wrote down his doubts about his own project in his diary, Thorsnes detailed his doubts and questions in his PhD thesis, asking whether he as an outsider could really engage artistically with the collective griefscape of another place.

When the audience walks in, the performance space is filled with chairs that all have notes on them. A video projection covers one entire wall, showing a seemingly idyllic landscape with lush green trees and bushes. Four performers wearing surgical gloves enter the space and start taking the notes from the chairs, placing them along the edges of the room. They eventually re-enter with their eyes closed, feeling their way through the space. Meanwhile, more footage is projected on top of the original video, this time showing war scenes and the unearthing of a mass grave. The physical language of the performers becomes more and more distorted. They balance on one leg, hop around, bump into the chairs, their upper bodies rocking from side to side. They start to empty the space, carrying the chairs on their backs with their bodies bent double. They crawl back into the space, as if through the trenches in a war zone. When only a few chairs are left, an older female performer sits down to rest and starts to sing a folk song in a nostalgic, soothing tone of voice. Her song is interrupted by a soundtrack that suggests explosions and mortar fire. The performers start running across the stage and ducking behind the remaining chairs. They walk in slow motion or jump over invisible obstacles. They alternate between frenetic, deformed movements of anxiety and moments in which their bodies freeze. Eventually, they all return to a more introspective state, closing their eyes and collapsing onto the floor.

They then get up again and perform more isolated, obsessive actions: singing a song, practicing folk dance steps, or repeating the same short monologue over and over again. A fifth performer in a wheelchair, who has been an invisible part of the audience until now, enters the stage and starts engaging with them, mirroring their movements or asking them to carry him around. By doing so, he pulls them out of their isolation, one by one. The performers start to invite the audience to participate in these gestures of physical support. Eventually, everyone ends up back in the space, walking slowly in a spiral pattern while holding hands. The community is brought together in a collective ritual of mourning. The performer in the wheelchair also evokes the memory of Thorsnes's friend Martin, whose death was the subject of the first, more personal part of the trilogy. Martin had a form of spinal muscular atrophy which meant that he had to move around in a wheelchair. In literally re-membering the exceptional physicality of his friend, Thorsnes creates a meaningful link between the individual and collective griefscapes of his pieces.

Taking an ethnographic approach to the analysis of his artistic research process, Thorsnes brings his own autobiography

into play. He grew up on a farm and was exposed to cycles of life
and death early on, particularly relating to the animals on the farm.
Killing and slaughtering were necessary parts of farm life and as
a child he often witnessed it. At the same time, he was kept away
from attending funerals and the adults in his life were not able to
share their mourning:

> I grew up in this what I now conceive a schizophrenic
> dichotomy: between an integral understanding of being part
> of the cycle of life with its death and dying on the one hand,
> and being marked by unmentioned and prolonged grieving
> on the other.[5]

Many visual artists have focused on collective mourning processes
in their work. There are iconic works such as Marina Abramović's
*Balkan Baroque*, her contribution to the 1997 Venice Biennale.
In the performance, Abramović sat on a pile of bloody cow
bones and scrubbed them one by one for four consecutive days,
while singing folk songs and laments from different regions of
the former Yugoslavia. Projected behind her was a video tryptic
depicting her between portraits of her mother and father.
Abramović had used the washing of bones (or skeletons) before,
for example in the performance series *Cleaning the Mirror* (1995).
They are re-enactments of the rituals of exhumation that are still
practiced in Greece.

    The South African visual artist and theater director William
Kentridge has often depicted (funeral) processions and laments in
his video installations. A recent example is the impressive installation, *More Sweetly Play the Dance* (2015), which he created for
the Eye Filmmuseum in Amsterdam. Eight large screens create
a 45-meter-long frieze in which a procession of lamenters passes
by in eternal cycles, accompanied by a funeral brass band. The
procession features a catalogue of people 'on the move,' evoking
streams of African refugees fleeing war or famine. 'The image of
a procession of people pulling or carrying their baggage is both a
contemporary and immediate image and one deeply rooted in our
psyches.'[6] Another of Kentridge's sources of inspiration was Walt
Disney's short animated film *The Skeleton Dance* (1929): 'This is
one of the great moments of animation history. ... The transformation the skeletons undergo suggests that all is possible.'[7] It inspired
him to create his own Dance of the Dead.

There is an irony of course in a dance both for and against death. Death as a dancer leading its companions to their end, and the medieval idea that if one danced furiously enough, if there was enough energy released in the making of the dance, one could keep death at bay.[8]

Besides *Vajtocja*, the video by the Albanian film and performance artist Adrian Paci discussed in the previous chapter, the exhibition *Mourning: On Loss and Change* at the Hamburger Kunsthalle also showed two more of his video works, both depicting collective processes of mourning. *Interregnum* (2017) is the more political work. The video consists of found footage of several state funerals in communist countries, including the funerals of Stalin and Mao. The images constantly switch between two expressions of mourning. On the one hand, there are choreographed public gestures of uniform, state-ordained grief, such as crowds queuing to salute the hearse, with people casting sideward glances or raising their fists. On the other hand, there are close-ups of more authentic, often extremely individual emotions that are experienced under the cover of a public crowd or in the privacy of someone's home, while watching or listening to the news on radio or television. The other work, *The Guardians* (2015), begins with stills depicting fragments of abandoned architecture interspersed with patches of nature (mostly weeds). Only very slowly do the images reveal that the video was shot in an abandoned cemetery. The only human presence is a group of children, who walk through it, sit on the gravestones, and play with the gravel. Their movements become more deliberate in their acts of care: hands are seen cleaning stones or pulling weeds. The final image shows a bird's eye view of the cemetery, revealing many 'little guardians' taking care of the graves. I was particularly touched by this video because it reminded me of my own visits to my father's grave and how very unemotional and pragmatic they usually were: just cleaning his gravestone or raking the sand.

Shortly after the 9/11 terrorist attacks, the Finnish artist Pia Lindman, who was living in New York City at the time, began collecting photographs of people who were grieving. They included news images from *The New York Times* taken at the World Trade Center in the aftermath of the attacks, but also photographs of women grieving over their dead in other wars, such as the Palestinian-Israeli and the Russian-Chechnyan conflicts.

She made drawings of the postures and physical gestures of grief in an attempt to re-enact and embody them. In a project entitled *Lakonikon*, she then performed these re-enactments in front of a camera. The videos show the process of her searching for the correct gestures and poses, creating a distancing effect. After filming the videos, she made a new series of drawing based on her own re-enactments, entitled *Black Square Drawings*. In these drawings, she traced stills from the videos in pencil. Eventually, she also started to give live performances of her re-enactments in public spaces, with the drawings spread out in front of her on music stands like a musical score. She performed in a window display in front of the Freedom of Expression National Monument in New York and on a guided tour of different monuments in Vienna, including Rachel Whiteread's Holocaust Memorial. Lindman says that doing these re-enactments triggered real emotions of grief in her.[9] Referring to Lindman's work, the MIT psychologist Sherry Turkle concludes that 'grief is always expressed in a set of structured patterns, programmed by biology and culture.'[10] It is these common patterns that allow for our mourning to be shared with others.

For Daniel Leader, an essential part of the 'the dialogue of mournings' is the transformation of mourning into a collective process. By sharing and witnessing it, we can better understand it and integrate our individual experiences into a greater whole. Linking individual experiences of mourning to a collective experience is also a key function of the traditional laments. Most Greek scholars highlight the importance of the *moiróghia* as a community-building practice that supports the members of the community through the shared act of witnessing. Alexiou states that the lamentation is considered 'a social duty for the whole community' and explains that the lamenters don't have to be invited by the bereaved family but 'simply come to the house and weep, first for whoever has died, then for their own dead.' She concludes that the ritual of the *moiróghia* is by its very nature 'dependent upon the collective participation of the whole community.'[11]

The Greek verb *martiráo* (μαρτυράω), means both 'to witness' and 'to suffer for.' In his anthropological field work, Varvantakis came across a lament that utilized both aspects of this word: '*witness her*, to acknowledge her existence in the kinship, and *suffer for her*, to properly express grief through the ritual of *kláma* and lamenting.'[12] Seremetakis in turn highlights how these inter-related notions of witnessing and suffering 'are narrative devices in laments that fuse jural notions of reciprocity and truth-claiming with the emotional nuances of pain.'[13]

I have reflected and written elsewhere[14] on the importance of the act of witnessing in contemporary discourses on performance. The idea originates in an essay by Bertolt Brecht, 'The Street Scene: A Basic Model for an Epic Theatre' (1950), in which he identifies the 'eyewitness' as his model not only for the spectator but also for the performer.

> For practical experiments I usually picked as my example of completely simple, 'natural' epic theatre an incident such as can be seen at any street corner: an eyewitness demonstrating to a collection of people how a traffic accident took place.[15]

This idea of the witness has been developed further by the British theater director Tim Etchells, founder of the performance collective *Forced Entertainment*. Referencing Chris Burden's description of his audience as witnesses, Etchells makes a distinction between merely being a spectator and being a witness:

> It's a distinction I come back to again and again and one which contemporary performance dwells on endlessly because to witness an event is to be present at it in some fundamentally ethical way, to feel the weight of things and one's own place in them, even if that place is simply, for the moment, as an onlooker.[16]

At the end of his discussion of the witness role, Tim Etchells refers to Brecht's street scene: 'We're left, like the people in Brecht's poem who've witnessed a road accident, still stood on the street corner discussing what happened, borne on by our responsibility to events.'[17] The dance scholar Ann Cooper Albright takes up this notion of responsibility, describing in her introduction to the book *Choreographing Difference: The Body and Identity in Contemporary Dance* (1997) how watching a performance of *La Tristeza Complice* by Alain Platel's les ballets C de la B transformed her from a spectator into a witness. She writes: 'To witness something implies a responsiveness, the response/ability of the viewer towards the performer.' Albright differentiates 'the consuming gaze' of the spectator who wants to be entertained from the act of witnessing, which is 'much more interactive, a kind of perceiving (with one's whole body) that is committed to a process of mutual dialogue.'[18] In one of her other essays, *Moving Contexts* (2001), Albright further develops this notion of witnessing as 'a shared responsibility.' She explains that witnessing has long been part of the Indian aesthetic of *rasa*, which 'is based on the notion of a mutual responsibility between the performer and the audience. ... in the sense of a real "responsiveness", an ability to "respond" to the energy of that moment.'[19] In a more recent analysis of a series of les ballets C de la B productions, *Being Alone Together* (2020), Albright continues to reflect on the act of witnessing, relating it also to Jean-Luc Nancy's discussion of 'with-ness' in *Being Singular Plural* (1995). The act of being moved, 'represents an intertwining of somatic feeling and political urgency.'[20]

It is my personal conviction that the original and core purpose of performance art (whether theater, dance, storytelling, or song) as a ritual practice lies in engaging one's community into the role of the witness. By doing so, one keeps alive the memory of the events that are being re-enacted and allows them to transform. The lament traditions are a good example of how audiences can be invited to witness, i.e., to share responsibility, and to respond to someone's personal grief. Through this process, the individual mourning process becomes a collective one.

I will allow myself to digress from my main topic here in order to reflect further on the witness role, which is in fact a key aspect of my work as a dramaturg (in which role I accompany other artists in their creative processes). Bringing the witness role into the studio as early as possible in the creation process is one of the most powerful things that dramaturgs can contribute. Through their silent, but felt, presence, they will influence the dialogue between the choreographer and performers in somatic and energetic ways.

This somatic and energetic potential of the witness role is not often mentioned in the literature on dance dramaturgy, but there are a few examples. In one of the most poetic descriptions of the work of a dance dramaturg I have found, the Slovenian dramaturg Eda Čufer describes how her first theatrical experiences consisted of witnessing the cutting of a tree and the killing of a pig on her parents' farm when she was a child.[21] Christel Stalpaert references the dramaturg Carmen Mehnert, who describes her work as a 'dialogue on an energy level.'[22] And Eleonora Fabião discusses energetic communication in her contribution to the *On Dramaturgy* issue of the journal *Women and Performance* (2003):

> I could explore a quality of interaction that interests me a lot, a kind of 'energetic communication.' It may seem abstract, but this way of acting upon someone is as concrete as it is effective. As some understandings can only be formulated through a good conversation, others can only be produced by this kind of interchange, through the intersection of energy and silent talk. You can energize and be energized (or stimulate and be stimulated) if you concentrate your attention. Actors and directors are particularly trained to work things out in this way. And, as I understood, dramaturgs can also take great advantage attending to this communicational strategy. If one of the most interesting specificities of the theatrical scene is the magnetic quality of present presences, the importance of investigating and generating energetic ways of communication seems obvious.[23]

As a dramaturg, I intuitively play with proximity and distance to the process, creating subtle shifts in the witness role that might influence the interaction on the floor between performers and choreographer. As the study of proxemics in the social sciences and in anthropology has revealed, it is not only the actual physical distance of the witness that can influence a situation, but also for instance the angle from which he or she is watching, or the level of focus and engagement in his or her gaze. In the early stages of a rehearsal process I also like to physically participate and experience the movement research in my own body. In the later stages, I am constantly exiting and re-entering the process. My felt presence or absence creates energetic shifts in the shared space and in our 'relationality,' which subtly influences the creative process.

The witness role involves a certain amount of patience and the ability to let things evolve without interfering. Hans-Thies Lehmann defines this as 'a sort of Heideggerian *Gelassenheit* ... the calmness to let things happen without imposing one's own ready-made concepts on a work in progress.'[24] The best moments in the process are when you, as the witness/dramaturg, are having a thought about how it should best continue, only for this to happen simultaneously on the floor or in the interaction between

choreographer and dancers, without you having to interfere or even pronounce that thought. These moments of synchronicity are always an indication that the process is on the right track.

As a dramaturg-witness, I support artists in their creative processes. Often these creative acts involve a letting go of past habits. 'Kill your darlings' is a common expression that is especially useful toward the end of the process, when the final editing takes place. Daniel Leader may state that the creative act is a powerful means of overcoming mourning, but it is also true that every creative act includes a necessary process of letting go, which in turn can cause grief and mourning.

An artist who has rigorously researched the role of the witness in her work is Tedi Tafel, a Canadian interdisciplinary movement artist whom I have accompanied as a dramaturg. Tedi combines a movement practice rooted in Authentic Movement with multi-media installations that are often presented outdoors in the urban landscape of Montréal, where she lives and works. Authentic Movement is a movement practice that was originally developed by Mary Starks Whitehouse as a movement therapy rooted in Jungian psychotherapy. In it, movements are generated by listening for and embodying internal impulses. To support this listening, you practice it with your eyes closed, while a partner/ witness is present to hold the space for you and provide safety through their open, non-judgmental attention. The witness also helps you remember your movements from a complementary perspective. Tedi has applied the main principles of this practice to her own work, developing it further by working with the same group of mature performers over a period of more than ten years. They practice listening to their own bodies, to each other, and to the urban environments they research and perform in. In 2014, Tedi created the project *Everyday*. In preparation of this, we sent each other letters as part of our dramaturgical-dialogical practice.

> Dear Guy,
> I feel ready to begin to write to you about this project I am creating, called *Everyday*. ... For *Everyday* I am interested in how performances can be inserted into the public space, so that the audience is able to see both the performance and the actions of the general public. I am asking the performers to be in a place of response, to allow the choice to come from where they are, from the architecture, design,

In her next work, *Crying in Public* (2018), Tedi continued to explore how a performance and its performers could make both the audience and the general public in a public space more aware—or differently aware—of their environment. But as the title suggests, this time the work also explicitly dealt with mourning. The trigger for the creation of *Crying in Public* was the death of her closest friend. Tedi's own mourning and her process of coming to terms with her friend's death led her on a spiritual quest, which nevertheless remained firmly rooted in material reality. 'What began as an interest in cycles of birth, death and regeneration has evolved into a more full expression of the spiritual dimension of the human condition. The universe is really inspired matter.'[26] *Crying in Public* describes communal lives and the resultant feelings of isolation and separateness that come from this lack.[27]

Tedi created a series of interconnected works of different lengths, which were presented in three-day cycles of three daily performances, each performed in different public spaces in the same neighborhood at dawn, dusk, and at night. Just as the traditional *moirológhia* utilize day and night as an evocative pair of opposites, Tedi carefully chose the times of day at which the performances took place. She describes dusk as being a liminal transition zone: 'Dusk is considered a time that fuses the material (day, light) and the spiritual (night, darkness). Night and day reflect the irrevocable dualism that was built in the cosmos. Dusk shows how these dualities can be transcended.'[28] People who had bought tickets got a map and a schedule and were invited to see as many performances as they wanted to. The performances had titles such as *Circles and Angels*, *Grief Map* or *A Day in the Life*. Tedi explored archetypal movement patterns and actions such as circling and spiraling, kneeling or lying down, which are all familiar from traditional celebrations such as the Greek *panegyria* described in the third chapter.

*Grief Map* uses the performers' personal expressions of grief to create 'an honest act of prayer or ritual.' It is performed in the basement of a church at night. Five people wander into the large, dark space, each carrying a blanket and a candle. The movements and actions of the dancers are very simple: a blanket is unfolded and laid carefully on the ground; a candle is lit; the performers walk the parameters of the blanket's edge, fall onto the blanket, and slowly roll side to side. After a while, the blanket is rolled up again and the candle is picked up and blown out while the performer starts walking.

> I see the movement through the space as a kind of mapping of the dancers' experiences ... The actions of lighting and extinguishing the flames in the darkness is intended to resemble the birth and death of stars poetically linking these deeply personal acts to cosmic occurrences.'[29]

The audience is invited to witness the proposals as 'intimate offerings,' which

> ...will summon your own participation not only with the dance (for the dance is only a part) but also with the place

and the time of the day and the weather and the other myriad contingencies of where we find ourselves.[30]

In his study *Trauma-Tragedy: Symptoms of Contemporary Performance* (2012), Patrick Duggan positions trauma-tragedy 'as a means by which society can engage in attempting to understand, contextualize and bear witness to its own social dramas and traumas.'[31] Referencing Peggy Phelan, Duggan defines trauma not as 'the encounter with death but as the ongoing *re*-experiencing of having survived it.'[32] Duggan describes how contemporary forms of tragedy are 'trying to embody and bear witness to trauma in an immediate way.'[33] He discusses a number of theater performances of the first decade of the twenty-first century, including works by Chris Burden, Sarah Kane, Romeo Castellucci, Franko B, and Forced Entertainment. Of the latter's works, he analyzes Sophie Calle's *Exquisite Pain* (2007), which is one of the few performances by the British collective that is based on an existing script. For *Exquisite Pain*, Calle collected a series of testimonies from different people, who all answered the question: 'When and where did you suffer most?' The answers range from 'lost loves to destructive relationships to the death of a father whose funeral the thirteen-year-old son was prevented by his family from attending.'[34]

In his discussion of *Exquisite Pain* Duggan focuses on the importance of the witness role, illustrating how the 'performance's aesthetic and ethical composition is a layering of what we might think of as witnessing levels.'[35] He dedicates an entire chapter to the 'processes of witnessing and testimony,' which create 'surprising yet "insistent" parallels and connections between trauma and performance,'[36] and references others, including Simon Shepherd, who defines theater as 'an art of bodies witnessed by bodies.'[37] Duggan also quotes contemporary psychiatrists who highlight the central role that being witnessed and bearing witness plays in healing trauma symptoms. Drawing on Malcolm Heath's discussion of Aristotelian catharsis, he argues that the performative testimony or re-enactment of trauma allows sufferers 'to mediate, think through or balance "unwanted" emotions.'[38] This balancing of emotions is also one of the key aspects of the traditional laments. It is one of the main reasons why mourning needs to be performed in front of an audience of witnesses.

In his recent study *Tragedy, The Greeks, and Us* (2019), Simon Critchley rejects this 'homeopathic view of catharsis.'

He does so on basis of his exegesis of Aristotle's *Poetics*, concluding that 'there is not a word to support it.'[39]

> The whole question of tragedy, indeed the whole question of poetry and its relation to philosophy, turns on how we understand the core concept of catharsis. ... So, is catharsis either purgation, purification, or transformation? The problem is that we simply do not know what Aristotle meant by catharsis.[40]

Because we cannot know, at least on the basis of the original text, Critchley prefers a 'minimalist understanding of Aristotelian catharsis,' following Jonathan Lear's view that 'tragedy provides a safe environment in which emotions are raised and then relieved. But this relief is nothing as dramatic as a sudden release of dark, repressed, pent-up passions, let alone their quasi-religious purification or moral transformation.'[41] Critchley performs a similar exegesis of Plato's *Republic*, concluding that the birth of Western philosophy 'requires the elimination of lamentation and laughter in equal measure, for they both threaten mastery of self with an emotional excess.'[42] He goes on to say that 'at the core of philosophy ... lies affect regulation, the rational ordering of emotion.'[43] Critchley's discourse, however, is predominantly textual. At the very end of his book, recalling a conversation with Isabelle Huppert, he admits that his concepts and ideas never quite manage to explain what happens on stage, in that moment when 'one enters a unique space that provides an unparalleled experience of sensory and cognitive intensity.'[44] Critchley's argument that rational philosophy is incompatible with 'the emotional excess' of laments also doesn't take into account the fact that the lament form itself is already a formal device crafted to both express and contain the emotions of grief.

Both Margaret Alexiou in *The Ritual Lament in Greek Tradition* and Gail Holst-Warhaft in *Dangerous Voices: Women's Laments and Greek Literature* discuss the relationship between the popular, mainly female, oral tradition of the *moirológhia* and the literary, dominantly male form of Greek tragedy. Almost all tragedies include laments in different forms, and one of the functions of the chorus is also to comment on these laments or those who are lamenting. It would take another book to analyze the role that laments play in Greek tragedy, especially if one intended to include examples of contemporary adaptations and stagings. Scholars such as Erika Fischer-Lichte (*Tragedy's Endurance: Performance of Greek Tragedies and Cultural Identity in Germany since 1980*, 2017) or Hans-Thies Lehmann (*Tragedy and Dramatic Theatre*, 2015) have already done much significant work in this area. I will only mention one example, which made a deep impression on me: Johan Simons' 1994 staging of *The Persians* by Aeschylus. It was performed by Simons' company TG Hollandia, which he co-founded and co-directed with the composer and musician Paul Koek. *The Persians* is not only the oldest surviving Greek tragedy, but it also consists almost entirely of a series of laments about the defeat of the Persians by the Greeks in the battle of Salamis (480 BC). Holst-Warhaft comments that *The Persians* 'seems to be less about the Persian defeat than about lament itself and its power to affect action on stage and audience reaction. In other words, lament is not only practiced in the text, it becomes thematised.'[45]

For their staging, Simons and Koek commissioned a new translation of the Greek text by the Dutch theater scholar Herman Altena, who specializes in ancient Greek theater and who based his translation on the rhythmical differences and correspondences between Greek and Dutch. In his introductory text to the new translation, he argues for a formal approach to Greek tragedy that takes its musical characteristics into account. 'Through its specific metric form and the related forms of diction (parlando, recitative or song), Greek tragedy has a strong formal character which is at the same time its power.' Altena continues to argue that 'a psychological interpretation narrows down the broad perspective' of Greek tragedy. He also illustrates how in the Greek text 'intensified emotion is expressed by formal changes: spoken metre changes into lyrical, spoken language changes into song. Powerful emotions are chained to a rigid metric pattern.'[46]

Using Altena's translation as a libretto, Paul Koek wrote a musical score for the play. In a letter to Altena, Koek characterizes *The Persians* as a true piece of music theater: 'First, the words become sound, then movement, and only then meaning: slow tempo horizontally, monotony vertically, rhythmically complex.'[47] The chorus, or Council of Persian Elders, was performed by three opera singers who sang the score, plus three old men—not professional actors but retired farmers. All the other parts were performed by only two actors. Elsie de Brauw played Queen Atossa, and Jeroen Willems played all the male roles including the messenger, the ghost of the old king Darius, and Xerxes,

the defeated king returning form the battlefield.[48] Theater critic
Johan Thielemans described Willems's performance and his
three distinct timbres for each of the three roles/monologues:
'his recalcitrant sing-song voice for the messenger to announce,
half-lamentingly and half-rebelliously, the defeat of the army.'
King Darius stammers, 'The voice is mere sound, the actor a
virtuoso.' When Xerxes returns in shame from the war in the
final scene, his lamentation is sung: 'Again there is a change
of style, since Willems transforms Koek's simple score into a
touching aria ... His high pitch expresses through its mere form
a strong interiorized suffering.'[49]

> Xerxes:
> Shed tears, tears of loss and lead me to the palace.
> Chorus:
> Aiai aiai anguish, anguish.
> Xerxes:
> Wail now, in response to me.
> Chorus:
> A miserable gift from the miserable to the miserable.
> Xerxes:
> Wail your song, tuned in to mine
> Chorus:
> Ototototoi,
> A heavy burden hit us
> Oi, it terribly hurts
> Xerxes:
> Strike, strike and moan for my sake.
> Chorus:
> My sorrow shed tears
> Xerxes:
> Wail, in response to me
> Chorus:
> I have reasons enough to be concerned
> Xerxes:
> Raise your voice and lament.[50]

The above fragment of Xerxes's lament at the end of *The Persians*
is another example of how laments combine language and
non-language (i.e., stylized cries and sobs). In *The Dominion of the
Dead* (2003), Robert Pogue Harrison discusses the same fragment

and the difficulties it poses for translators who need to find an adequate expression for this 'voice of grief.'

> Where the English interjects words like 'alas,' 'woe' and 'anguish,' the Greek features a variety of wailings sounds. In those primitive howls, which translators generally do not know what to do with, we hear echoes of the stammering voice of grief prior to its articulation in discrete words.[51]

For Harrison, Xerxes' lament supports his thesis that 'it was perhaps through grief that the human voice gained its first articulations.'[52]

When it was presented as part of the Ghent edition of the 1995 Dutch-Flemish Theater Festival, I saw TG Hollandia's *The Persians* several times in a row. In the same festival, two other contemporary performances also explicitly referenced laments. The Dutch theater director Gerardjan Rijnders staged a choreographed version of Jeremiah's *Lamentations* with Toneelgroep Amsterdam, and the Ghent-based theater director Erik De Volder and composer Dick Van der Harst (with whom I would later discover the *moirológhia* in Epirus) created *Diep in het bos* (Deep in the Forest, *1995*), in which a chorus of seven women lament the collective Belgian trauma of the Dutroux child abuse murders. The songs that Dick van der Harst wrote for *Diep in het Bos* draw on the Breton tradition of *gwerziou*, in which groups of women sing a capella, commenting in an antiphonic way on the gloomy events in their daily lives, including the death of children, murder and betrayals. In this particular case, the Breton music sounds like dance music, its happy melodies offering a striking counterpoint to the horrible stories told by the lyrics.

At the time, all of TG Hollandia's work was site-specific. For this production, they had chosen an abandoned industrial site formerly occupied by ACCEC factories in the harbor of Ghent. During one of the performances, a thunderstorm broke out and the rain poured down through the broken roof onto the stage. During Xerxes's final lament, Jeroen Willems stood drenched in a violent rain shower, his voice becoming both amplified and erased by the downpour. The sky was crying with him.

*The Persians* is less frequently staged by theater directors than other Greek tragedies. In Greece, there have been a number of

iconic productions: Karolos Koun staged it in 1966, on the eve of the Greek dictatorship. Theodoros Terzopoulos's 2006 production was booed when it opened the Epidaurus festival because he used a mixed Greek-Turkish cast and also alternated between the two languages. What these productions have in common is that they place great emphasis on the chorus and its collective voice, highlighting the formal musicality of the play.

Referencing Julia Kristeva, Hans-Thies Lehmann in his book *Tragedy and Dramatic Theatre* (2015) defines Greek tragedy as 'a polylogue' in which 'voices are split up': '... the voice of the protagonists, the singing of the chorus, the message of the Messenger, dialogue, prayer, lament, dirge.' Citing Anton Bierl, he argues that *The Persians* is about 'making pain communal in the mourning rituals of the chorus.'[53] In an Open University educational video, theater scholar Edith Hall summarizes it even more succinctly: 'It is incredibly simple. In fact, very little happens. You have a community, which learns some bad news and it weeps.'[54]

The Irish theater and opera director Conor Hanratty saw Terzopoulos's staging of *The Persians* in Epidaurus and recognized in the musicality of the Greek vernacular a kinship with his own Irish tongue. *The Persians* had been performed in Ireland in English but never in Irish, so Hanratty took it upon himself to stage the play in Irish. He asked the contemporary Irish poet Nuala Ní Dhomhnaill to make a new translation and gathered a team of actors and musicians. Unfortunately, due to the Covid-19 lockdown, the premiere, which had been scheduled for the 2020 Dublin Theatre Festival, had to be postponed. Instead, Hanratty produced *PERSIANS—The Podcast*,[55] a series of ten episodes in which he guides listeners through the different parts of the play. He discusses aspects of the play's performance history, outlining a 'blueprint' for future performances. His erudite comments are interspersed with actors reading fragments of the Irish version. In the final episode, the Irish singer Iarla Ó Lionáird sings his version of Xerxes's lament. 'Xerxes is at the limits of human emotions. A register where words alone cannot communicate. He sings throughout because he is suffering. His extremity demands a bigger sound.'[56] Hanratty also notes the strong parallels between Greek laments and the Irish tradition of *caoinadh* (keening). 'This has echoes in the call and response of certain Irish rhythms and traditions.'[57]

In 2019, I was invited to the Light Moves Festival in Limerick, Ireland, by the festival's curators, the choreographer Mary Wycherley and the composer Jürgen Simpson, to present my work and research on the *moiróghia*. To prepare for this presentation, I began to research the Irish tradition of *caoineadh* (keening), which is similar to the Greek tradition of *moirológhia*. The Irish sound practitioner Michelle Collins completed an MA thesis on the subject, entitled 'Caoine: Spaces for Vocalising Grief. The de-ritualisation and re-ritualisation of keening in contemporary Ireland' (2014). In it she describes how the tradition of keening came under pressure from the combined forces of the Catholic Church, increased urbanization, and twentieth-century modernization, causing it to almost completely disappear. A similar thing happened to the *moirológhia*. Today, keening is again being researched by scholars and revived by artists. It is also being explored by health practitioners in the context of therapeutic, community-oriented work.[58] In addition to her thesis, Collins produced a radio documentary on the topic for Irish National Radio: *The Sounds of Grief: The Practice and Tradition of Caoineadh*.[59]

In both the documentary and her thesis, Collins explains that keening has been a predominantly female tradition. References to it can be traced back as far the pre-Christian era, when it appears in stories about the Irish goddess Brighd. Traditionally, keening was performed by the *bean chaointe* or keening woman. In the third chapter we saw how Seremetakis describes the *moirológhia* as 'transgressive sanctuaries' for women, in which they are free to comment on and critique dominant male institutions. Collins in turn describes how,

> ...for the duration of the mortuary rituals the *bean chaointe* was seen as half-mad and in this state was able to publicly voice and criticize often private matters such as abusive husbands, or public issues like harsh colonizers or priests. This was the one situation afforded to women where they could use their voice and be heard without constraint.[60]

The *caoineadh* is 'a two-fold, texted weeping,' which consists of three parts: a salutation or address to the dead (which resembles a mantra), the actual dirge or lament, and the gol or cry, which is typically written as *Och-ochóne*. Just like the *moirológhia*, the *caoineadh* are improvised compositions 'created by combining and recombining traditional motifs, from a body of stock phrases, according to a traditional metre called *rosc*.'[61] One of Collins's field interlocutors describes the change in pitch of the cry as the essence of the keen, 'which changed the balance and allowed listeners to release grief.'[62] This release of grief by moving the listeners to tears—and thereby literally 'liquefying' grief—is one of the main functions of the *caoineadh*. Its other, more spiritual, task is to accompany the deceased's spirit on his or her journey to the land of the dead. Collins also gives an overview of literary sources describing the physical language that accompanies the *caoineadh*. She references Angela Bourke's study *Keening as Theatre: J.M. Synge and the Irish Lament Tradition* (2000), which states that the keener's performance was as 'theatrical as it was vocal.'[63]

> The performative aspects of keening were striking. ... Keening women, covered in long black shawls and dressed in often torn skirts, rocked their body, from the base of the spine, to and fro, with arms apart clapped hands, beat their chests with their fists. ... Bourke suggests the keening women seemed to have taken their 'metre from the rhythm of her body's movement, and may very well have used the rocking and repetition to induce an altered stated of consciousness.'[64]

In Limerick I met the Irish singer and interdisciplinary artist Ceara Conway, who uses the Irish tradition of *caoineadh* in her contemporary vocal artistic practice. In an unpublished lecture, Ceara discusses how songs 'can act as conduits for embodying the pain of others, and thus be considered agents for empathy and change.'[65] *Making Visible* (2014) is a ritual performance made with and for a group of women seeking asylum in Ireland, who were caught in the Direct Provision system that provided them with a government stipend of less than 20 Euros per week but prohibited any kind of work or access to education. In order to make this inhumane system 'visible,' Ceara created a public performance that consisted of three laments in different traditions. First, Veronica Ncube, one of the asylum seekers, sang an old gospel lament in her native language of Xhosa, lamenting the deaths of her son and husband and the impossibility of visiting their graves. This was then followed by Ceara greeting the audience and telling them that many years ago in Ireland

> when someone had died or when a sad event had taken place, the *bean chaointe* would go to the highest point of the village and would wail as a way of letting people know that a death had occurred and as a signal for the community to come together in an act of solidarity.

Ceara would continue stating: 'I am bringing attention to the fact that something very sad is happening in our own community in Galway City' and then she and other members of the community would give testimonies, highlighting the atrocities of the Direct Provision System. In between the testimonies two other Irish laments were sung, one of which (*Cáit Ní Ghallchóir*) also expresses a mother's grief over the death of her son.

> And o woe!
> And my child
> What will I do?
> You are gone from me
> And o woe!
> And last year
> I have no body
> And o woe!
> I am alone
> If I had you early in the morning
> Och, Och, o woe, without you[66]

These laments were sung by Veronica, Ceara, and the Irish singer Nóirin Ní Rian. When *Making Visible* was performed in a church in Galway, Ceara asked the audience to stand in a circle, in close proximity to the singers, to highlight the collective experience of witnessing. 'They could see each other's emotional responses such as crying, looking moved, or for that matter, uncomfortable or bored expressions.'[67]

The Flemish choreographer Koen Augustijnen has two main sources of inspiration: music on the one hand, and visual sources such as films or photographs on the other. The trigger for his production *Ashes* (2009) was a World Press photograph showing the aftermath of the Pinatubo volcano eruption in the Philippines.

In the photograph, the entire landscape has turned ash gray, with ash from the volcano covering every single building and tree. A solitary woman walks through this monochromatic landscape, coloring it with her blue dress and bright red umbrella. The umbrella seems like a futile attempt at protection from the ash downpour. For Augustijnen, the image prompted questions about how we as humans deal with the aftermath of a catastrophe. What survival strategies do we have to re-build society? Ashes are traces of destruction but they also fertilize the soil for a new cycle: death and rebirth. Out of his original questions grew new ones: How do you react to an environment that changes drastically? How can you let go of things? How do you say goodbye? What are people willing to do to hold on to things?

Koen is a choreographer who can easily invent hundreds of choreographic tasks on a given theme. Here are some of the tasks he set for himself and his dancers, using the above questions as starting points for improvisations and movement research:

— Three experiences where you experienced that 'nothing is forever'
— Fight your demons
— What do you miss?
— Everyone for her/himself
— A memory from childhood
— Desperately looking for contact
— Melancholy
— A group that falls apart
— Try to displace your heart
— To bring the body back to life from a dead position
— To guide someone who is blind.

The last task was inspired by the Nobel laureate José Saramago's novel *Blindness* (1997), which had recently been made into a film by Fernando Meirelles. *Blindness* depicts the struggle for survival after a city has been hit by a mysterious plague that turns everyone blind. Two other films also became important sources for *Ashes*: Michael Haneke's *Le temps du loup* (2003), which depicts a group of survivors in a rural environment after an unspecified cataclysm, and Leo Carax's *Les Amants du Pont-Neuf* (1991).

The opening of *Ashes* recreates the image of the original world press photo. A streetlight illuminates the stage, revealing dancers in immobile, statuesque positions, spread out across a monochromatic gray landscape. One dancer dressed in blue and carrying a red umbrella walks among them and begins to dance a solo that resembles a person hyperventilating and going through fits of hysteria. Her aliveness activates the other performers, who begin to reposition themselves or drag each other across the stage, still in a state of seeming apathy.

For the music, Koen Augustijnen collaborated with the countertenor Steve Dugardin and the composer Wim Selles, to select a baroque repertoire of arias and pieces by Händel. These are performed live on stage by two singers and musicians playing traditional instruments such as the lute and the cello, as well as more unusual instruments such as the marimba and the accordion. At the end of the opening scene, we hear the voice of the counter-tenor singing dispersed fragments, while the marimba player introduces a rhythm for a second dancer's solo. Starting from his hands, the dancer builds up frenetic twists in his body, expressing a sense of being lost. The marimba melody develops into a percussive climax, at which point all the dancers begin to run aimlessly, one of them even crashing into a wall. Eventually, they start hitting themselves and each other in a vain attempt to clean themselves of the gray dust. An aftershock? Or a memory of the original catastrophe? Throughout the piece, the dancers' solos express their own sense of being lost. They alternate between a more dramatic, tragic mode and a lighter, comical tone. A dancer/acrobat enacts a series of falls from different heights and reveals that a trampoline has been built into the two-story building dominating the set. Later he will gather all the other performers around him to create an imaginary grave, in which he lies down to hold his own funeral speech: 'My last words. What are you looking at? Leave me. Look at yourself. You are a bunch of sadness.'[68]

Interspersed among the solos are a series of duets, all inspired by the relationships in the film *Les Amants du Pont-Neuf*. They depict variations of longing and separation, and the power imbalances that result when different levels of dependence are re-vealed. Again, drama and comedy are closely intertwined, such as in a duet where a female dancer calls her male partner in a repetitive cycle of 'Viens et pars!' ('Come. Leave.') *Ashes* ends with a long group sequence in which the dancers spiral around themselves and the singer. They form a chorus to support a single dancer, who is dancing a final solo while blindfolded, trying to find directions.

Initially, Koen had landed on these circular, spiral-like movement patterns rather intuitively, but he then continued to use and develop them more consciously, also including them in workshops as a way to build trust in a group. He calls them 'the cosmos': 'Each person is a planet that circulates around other people/planets.'[69] The solo ends with the performer creating a wailing sound on the mouthpiece of a clarinet. One by one, all the dancers lie down on the stage and start creating repetitive rolling movements resembling waves, from which they occasionally rise up. This final, relentless movement is accompanied by an excerpt of Händel's cantata HWV 197: *Ma se l'alma sempre geme, nell'amor arse e consunta* (If the soul is melancholic, love will be hard and all consuming).

I have already spoken about how artists frequently link their personal mourning processes to larger, more collective experiences of grief and mourning. With the creation of *Ashes*, the opposite happened. Koen Augustijnen had originally wanted to address the collective trauma of a community dealing with the aftermath of a natural disaster. But in the end, something happened that made the theme much more personally relevant. Just before the start of the rehearsal process for *Ashes*, Koen's father died unexpectedly. The funeral speech mentioned above rendered his father last words. Koen began creating the piece while still in the early, intense stages of his own mourning process. His vulnerability made the process more difficult, but it also gave rise to a sensitivity that remained vibrantly alive in the final result.

In the summer following the creation of *Ashes*, Koen, his partner Rosalba Torres Guerrero, and the dramaturg of les ballets C de la B, Hildegard De Vuyst, traveled to Ramallah in the occupied West Bank to work with Palestinian dancers and performers on the creation of a new piece, *Badke* (2013). *Badke* draws on the traditional Arabic dabke dance, using it as the starting point for a contemporary dance theater performance that celebrates joy as a form of resilience. Christel Stalpaert discusses *Badke* in her contribution to the book *The Choreopolitics of Alain Platel's les ballets C de la B* (2020), stating that '*Badke* should not be regarded as melancholic aesthetic, merely communicating a longing for a lost home,' but that the dancers 'engage with the losses and burdens of the pasts and presents in order to generate new opportunities for the future.'[70]

When *Badke* was presented at the 2014 Kalamata Festival in Greece, the Greek dramaturg Georgina Kakoudaki invited

Koen and Rosalba to consider embarking on a similar project and artistic journey, this time researching the traditional music and dances of Greece. In parallel to this, I introduced Koen and Rosalba to the Greek tradition of the *moiróghia*. We all shared a long history of affinity with Greek culture, having participated in the Summer Academies held by the Greek National Theatre (see also 'The Greek *moirológhia*'). Koen and Rosalba made several research trips to Greece, first to Crete and eventually to Epirus, where they found in Xanthoula Dakovanou, the artistic director of the Kerasova music festival, another inspired and knowledgeable collaborator. Xanthoula is a Greek musician and singer who has been working within the tradition but also allows it to transform and become attuned to contemporary sensitivities. As well as a musician, she is a doctor in psychoanalysis and a music therapist, with a great belief in the therapeutic potential of music.

With Koen and Rosalba as the core artistic team, we embarked on the creation process for a new piece, *Lamenta*, which was due to premiere in Avignon in the summer of 2020. Rehearsals with a group of nine Greek dancers began in Athens in March 2020. But after just one week, the first Covid-19 lockdown was announced and the team had no option but to stop rehearsals. Koen and Rosalba returned to Brussels while the dancers self-isolated in their respective homes all over Greece. In order to keep the group together and utilize our newly formed collective as a means of support, we moved the rehearsal process online. Koen and Rosalba gave the dancers individual tasks, which they filmed and sent back to Brussels for feedback. Weekly Zoom meetings were held to check in with each other and share the difficulties and insights arising from each individual's work.

One of the tasks that Rosalba proposed was inspired by the Japanese concepts of *honne* and *tatamae*. She asked the dancers to develop two distinctive movement qualities based on these two ideas. *Honne*, which literally means 'true sound,' refers to a person's true feelings. It is more interiorized, while *tatamae*, which translates as 'built in front' or 'façade,' describes a person's exteriorized public behavior. Both are considered important in Japanese culture and are understood as complementary aspects of experience and social behavior that need to be kept in balance. In a similar way, the laments are a way of exteriorizing the at times extreme emotions of grief in a codified and shared musical language, which both supports and contains their expression.

With Xanthoula as musical director, a group of fifteen Greek musicians gathered to create new recordings of the *moirológhia* selected for the piece. The musicians included the renowned Epirus clarinetist Nikos Filippidis and his band, the Epirote percussionist and singer Alexandros Rizopoulos, numerous musicians of the contemporary, Greek ethno-jazz scene as well as Xanthoula herself as a singer. The Greek musicians were joined by the French jazz musician and flute virtuoso Magic Malik. *Lamenta* begins with Μαριόλα (Mariola), a traditional *moirolói* from Epirus that is often played at the beginning or end of the *panegyria*, the local village feast.

> Poor Mariola, rise from the earth.
> Rise from the black soil; you are my heart, Mariola
>
> How can I rise without feet, poor woman?
> How can I touch without hands?
>
> You are my soul, Mariola.
> Use your nails, make them shovels
> Use your palms and make them cups.
> You are my soul, Mariola.
> Throw the black ground to one side.
> Throw the gravestone to the other side and rise.
> You are my soul, Mariola.
>
> Herbs are growing on my grave.
> Come and clean it and shed black tears
> And then maybe you can resurrect me[71]

Forming a counterpoint to the glissando of the lament, the dancers perform a rhythmic and percussive dance involving clapping of hands and stamping of feet. While they connect rhythmically in the horizontal plane, their bodies appear to be pulled down by gravity to the point of collapse. Eventually, the oldest dancer separates from the group to perform a solo expressing his emotions, while the group continues to support him as a chorus, their bodies swaying and swooning in an up-and-down motion. The lyrics of the accompanying song describe a father letting go of his son who is emigrating (see also next chapter). This opening scene creates a state of suspension, a rhythmic and temporal in-between state that is maintained for most of the performance, until the cathartic release of the final section. The sense of suspension is also present in the bodies of the performers, their torsos often bent forward or backward, with arms or legs raised or lifted.

Throughout the performance, the group/chorus supports individual performers in energetic and rhythmic ways, acting as witnesses to their expressions. In Greek slang, these solo moments are referred to as *dalgas* (Νταλκάς) a word derived from Turkish and meaning 'wave.' It was probably introduced into the Greek vernacular as part of the *rebetika* tradition, which has its roots in Asia Minor and the exodus of its Greek population following the destruction of Smyrna. It refers both to the intoxication and the depressive aftermath of a 'high' from drugs and to the inner pain and sorrow caused by unrequited love. A group of witnesses supporting the *dalgas* of one of their own is still very much alive in Greek culture. I have observed the phenomenon many times, not only during the village celebrations but even in Athens discotheques. Seeing it reminded me of Nadia Seremetakis' description of the traditional laments as a dialogue between 'a chorus of *moirolyistres* generating antiphonic responses to the *koriféa*, "the soloist in pain."'[72] In the polyphonic singing of Epirus, the *partis* starts the song. S/he is supported by the *isokrates* and *klostis*, who support her individual expression of pain with droning sounds and harmonies, respectively. When one song finishes, another *partis* takes over and starts a new song. The group will continue this process until everyone who has felt the need has been allowed to perform their mourning and express their pain.[73]

For the chorus, Koen and Rosalba have adapted different variations on the circular, spiraling 'cosmos' movement patterns that Koen had already started using in *Ashes*. The artists see an analogy between this pattern and traditional Greek dances, which also often use the circle or the spiral, 'in order to connect and to generate more energy.'[74] The group alternates its rhythms, slowing down and accelerating at different times and varying its energy level in a way that is not dissimilar to the energetic S-curve Barbara Raes uses in her rituals (see previous chapter).

Occasionally, the support of the group is replaced by a more individualized form of support: in a series of duets, bodies reach out to prevent each other from collapsing or to pull each other up. In another reference to Greek dances, this is often done with the help of a handkerchief. In the Greek *panegyria*, the handkerchief gives the soloist leading the line dance more freedom to express herself, while keeping her connected with the group, almost like an umbilical cord. With *Lamenta*, Koen and Rosalba want to create 'a mourning ritual where people individually and collectively go through waves of intense physical expressions of their grief. This process is repetitive and its cyclical aspect is an important part of the overall dramaturgy.'[75]

While the spiral is at the heart of the physical expression of this mourning process, the musical dramaturgy of the piece is constructed around a series of Epirote *moirológhia*. They describe different experiences of grief, from the death of a partner to separation through exile, and from a violent death by murder to a tragic death of drowning. After giving grief its space and allowing the mourning to be performed, the final fifteen minutes of the piece, a section entitled *Charos*, becomes an energetic celebration of life. The lyrics talk about death visiting earth and telling people to eat, drink, and celebrate.

> Drink and eat, everyone!
> For he who goes to the other world, will not come back.[76]

# Notes


1 Dillard 2017, p. 92.
2 Thorsnes 2015, p. 7.
3 Ibid., p. 31.
4 Ibid., p. 32.
5 Ibid., p. 41.
6 Kentridge 2015, p. 25.
7 Ibid., p. 17.
8 Ibid., p. 48.
9 See also: pialindman.com/backup/ Review/nytpdf/Art_Terror_lindman. pdf.
10 Turkle 2011, p. 137.
11 Alexiou 1974, 2002, p. 50.
12 Varvantakis 2013, p. 148.
13 Seremetakis 1991, p. 102.
14 See Cools 2017.
15 Brecht 1950, n.p.
16 Etchells 1999, p. 17.
17 Ibid., p. 18.
18 Albright 1997, p. xxii.
19 Albright 2001, p. 50.
20 Albright 2020, p. 73.
21 See Čufer 1997.
22 Stalpaert 2009, p. 123.
23 Fabião 2003, p. 32.
24 Lehmann and Primavesi 2009, p. 6.
25 Unpublished, personal letter from Tedi Tafel, 23 July, 2014. See also: vimeo.com/146718000?ut m_source=email&utm_medium=vime o-cliptranscode-201504&utm_ campaign=29220.
26 From the program text of *Crying in Public*.
27 Ibid.
28 From Tedi Tafel's unpublished personal notes.
29 Ibid.
30 From the program text of *Crying in Public*.
31 Duggan 2012, p. 8.
32 Ibid., p. 29.
33 Ibid., p. 42.
34 Ibid., p. 106.
35 Ibid., p. 108.
36 Ibid., p. 88.
37 Ibid., p. 89.
38 Ibid. p. 95.
39 Critchley 2019, pp. 256–259.
40 Ibid., pp. 187–188.
41 Ibid., p. 191.
42 Ibid., p. 150.
43 Ibid., p. 169.
44 Ibid., p. 279.
45 Holst-Warhaft 1992, 1995, p. 131.
46 Altena 1994, pp. 28–29: 'In de Griekse tekst wordt verhoogde emotie uitged-rukt door formele veranderingen. Gesproken metra gaan over in lyrische: spreektaal gaat over in zang. Krachtige emoties zijn geketend aan een strak metrisch patroon.'
47 Koek in Altena 1994, p. 45: 'Die woorden worden klank, dan beweging en dan betekenis: langzame tempi horizontaal, monotonie verticaal, ritmisch complex.'
48 Jeroen Willems was one of the most talented Dutch actors of his generation, both on stage and in films. Unfortunately, he died in 2012 at the too young age of 50.
49 Johan Thielemans in *Etcetera*, Ed 13; no. 50, p. 44.
50 Altena 1994, pp. 86–87.
  Xerxes: Laat tranen, tranen stromen van leed, ga richting paleis.
  Koor: Aiai aiai ongeluk ongeluk.
  Xerxes: Roep luid nu als mijn tegenstem.
  Koor: Rampzalige gift van ramp-zaligen aan rampzaligen.
  Xerxes: Schreeuw uit uw lied, in een cadans.
  Koor: Otototototoi, Een zware last, wat ons hier treft. Oi, wat doet mij dit vreselijk pijn.
  Xerxes: Blijf doorslaan, doorslaan en slaak zuchten van mij.
  Koor: Bedroefd als ik ben laat ik tranen stromen.
  Xerxes: Roep luid nu als mijn tegenstem.
  Koor: Ik heb redenen genoeg om bekommerd te zijn, mijn heer.
  Xerxes: Verhef nu uw stem met jammerklachten.
51 Harrison 2003, p. 68.
52 Ibid., p. 62.
53 Lehmann 2015, pp. 237–238: 'Es geht um die Kommunalisierung des Leids im chorischen Trauerritual.'
54 See: www.youtube.com/watch?v=vu gB9semEA8.
55 See: www.persiansthepodcast.com/.
56 Hanratty in *Persians: The Podcast: Episode 10: The Lament*.
57 Ibid.
58 For the latter see e.g., www.keening-wake.com.
59 See, soundcloud.com/the-lyric-feature/ the-sounds-of-grief.
60 Collins 2014, p. 24.
61 Ibid., p. 28.
62 Ibid., p. 29.
63 Bourke in Collins 2014, p. 31.
64 Collins 2014, p. 31.
65 Conway, unpublished lecture.
66 Caoineadh Cáit Ní Ghallchóir,

pre-Christian Lament, transcribed
by Nóirin Ní Rian and translated by
Ceara Conway:
    Cáit Ní Ghallchóir
    (I)s airiú
    Agus a leanbh
    Cad a dhéanfaidh me
    Tá tú ar s(h)iúl uaim
    (I)s airiú
    Agus an uiridh
    Níl duin ar bith agam
    (I)s airiú
    Agus mé liom féin
    Da mbeith eá go mocha gam
    Agus och, och, (I)s airiú gan thú

67    Conway, unpublished lecture.
68    From the performance text of *Ashes*.
69    From a personal email from Koen
Augustijnen, December 22, 2020.
70    Stalpaert 2020, p. 238.
71    Traditional lament form Epirus,
translation Xanthoula Dakovanou:
    Μαριόλα
    Ωρέ σήκω, Μαριόλα η μαύρη
    ν›από τη γη
    ωρέ κι από το μαύρο χώμα,
    ψυχή, καρδούλα μου
    Ωρέ με τι ποδάρια η μαύρη να
    σκωθώ
    ωρέ και χέρια ν›ακουμπήσω,
    ψυχή Μαριόλα μου
    Ωρέ κάνε τα νύχια σου τσαπιά,
    ωρέ τις απαλάμες φτυάρια,
    ψυχή, καρδούλα μου
    Ωρέ ρίξε το χώμα από μεριά,
    ωρέ την πλάκα `πο την άλλη,
    ψυχή, Μαριόλα μου
    Ωρέ το μνήμα μ' εχορτάριασε,
    ωρέ κι έλα να βοτανίσεις, ψυχή,
    Μαριόλα μου
    Ωρέ να χύσεις μαύρα δάκρυα,
    ωρέ κι ίσως και μ' αναστήσεις.

72    Seremetakis 1991, p. 99–100.
73    From a personal email from
Xanthoula Dakovanou, January 4,
2021.
74    From a personal email from Koen
Augustijnen, December 21, 2020.
75    Ibid.
76    Traditional song form Epirus,
translation Xanthoula Dakovanou:
    Φάτε, πιείτε, όλοι βρε παιδιά
    όποιος πάει στον άλλο κόσμο
    δεν ξαναγυρνά.

# Laments of Exile and Migration

> My far-away, exiled bird
> My poor estranged one
> And distressed one
> The foreign lands enjoy you
> And I am left with my sorrow
> What should I send you
> In those foreign lands?
> An apple would rot
> A rose would wither
> I send my tear
> In a golden handkerchief
> My scathing tear
> Burned the handkerchief.[1]

The Greek *moirológhia* are not only used to lament the dead, but also those who are absent for a longer period of time and are missed by their loved ones: a son who is doing his compulsory military service, for example, or a daughter who marries and moves elsewhere, or relatives who have emigrated. The experience of migration is captured by the Greek term *xenitia*, which 'refers to foreign or distant lands and the loneliness of living a life of exile there.'[2] Over the centuries, a large part of the Greek population has emigrated in several waves, some for economic, others for political reasons. 'We shouldn't forget that the majority of the population of Epirus left as immigrants and went to America, Europe, Australia, and Canada. This loss is also a kind of death, and as Greeks, we carry it in us.'[3]

The photographic essay by the Greek photographer Alexander Tsiaras that inspired Loring M. Danforth's study *The Death Rituals of Rural Greece* documents the tragic story of Thanasis, a young man who leaves his village to go and work in the United States for seven years. 'During this time his mother had begged him repeatedly to come back to Greece to see his family. Living abroad for so long was almost like being dead.'[4] Eventually he returns to Greece to get married, but upon his arrival in Athens, he is taken into custody in order to serve his compulsory military service. Three months into his army service, he dies in a car accident and only returns home in a coffin. 'Because Thanasis had never married, his funeral was celebrated "like a wedding." A white wedding crown was placed on his head, and wedding songs were sung over his body as funeral laments.'[5]

Almost every Greek family has relatives living abroad. Before the era of internet communication, the Greek laments were also a way of entering into dialogue with those who had emigrated and whose absence was felt. Even today, it is a way of expressing emotions that are evoked by this absence. In *Lamenta*, Koen Augustijnen and Rosalba Torres Guerrero also use *xehorismata*, a lament of a father saying goodbye to his son who is going abroad for work. Two pairs of opposites are placed in relationship with each other: life and death, and home and *xenitia*.

> Now that we get separated, come, my son, kiss me
> Because, between life and death, we do not know when we will meet again
> Come, I tell you, don't torture me, I am crying
> Ah, you are there and I am here. I am surprised my son, how we can live like that
> Oh, help us, Christ and Virgin Mary, so that the two of us meet again
> You are my beloved half, come, I am waiting for you.[6]

The fear of dying abroad, far from family and relatives, is a recurring topic in the *moirológhia* addressing exile and migration. The most feared scenario is the idea of dying in a place where there is nobody to properly mourn your death, or for a family member's death to remain 'uncried.' The Covid-19 crisis and its attendant travel restrictions, as well as the sudden strict limitations on gatherings of people, have exacerbated this fear. It is clear that when mourning processes cannot take their course, there are consequences for those left behind. Early on in the lockdown, several articles in *The New York Times* addressed this fact. One of them, entitled *How the Virus Robs Families of the Rituals of Mourning*,[7] describes the problems that arise when family members are not able to attend to their dying relatives and when funeral rites are extremely restricted or even suspended.

The American choreographer Mark Tompkins's solo *Stayin Alive (à ma mere)* (2018) recounts his frustrations and the emotional turmoil he experienced when his mother lay dying at home in the US while he was working in Europe. In the solo, Tompkins sits behind a table and addresses his mother directly: 'Mom, do you hear me. I am very sorry that I couldn't come earlier. I love you. I know she can hear me and waits for me.' He goes on to sing a number of popular songs for her in his distinctive cabaret style, including *Stayin' Alive* by the Bee Gees and *I Would Die 4 U* by Prince. He also reflects on his own aging process while trying to cross an imaginary border control point, theatrically suggested by a simple but effective set composed of a table, chairs, and a few airport barriers.

When the British-Brazilian choreographer Jean Abreu came to visit me in Vienna for the first time to discuss a potential collaboration, he told me the story of his brother who had died in a car accident after Jean had already emigrated from Brazil to London to pursue his career as a dancer. Jean missed his brother's funeral. Later, he had to relive the event when he returned home to take care of the formalities surrounding his brother's death (such as obtaining a death certificate and collecting insurance documents), because his parents were too devastated to deal with such things themselves. As we advanced in the creation process of what was to become *Solo for Two* (2018), other autobiographical stories were added to this central story. Jean looked back on his life as a series of journeys: first the daily bicycle ride to school, then the consecutive bus trips from Imperatriz to Belém and from Belém to Rio to pursue his dancing career, passing through five different provinces, each with their distinct landscapes. And eventually the regular flights between London and Brazil. The recurring ritual of saying goodbye. His father, who would keep insisting that he pack his suitcase. His mother, who would cry and hide in his suitcase the tastes and smells of home: coconut oil and cassava powder. Jean realized that his life's journey had been an endless series of endings and new beginnings. 'The intensity of revisiting my parents swings between as if I never left, to having never arrived or even not being from here, at all.'[8]

Although we didn't use these autobiographical stories in a literal way in the piece, they were nevertheless the emotional soil on which *Solo for Two* grew. We looked at how loss is embodied in the experience of the migrant, who doesn't have a fixed point of origin but whose journey through life is an infinite series of endings and new beginnings. We also discovered that loss is not only a negative experience, but also has the potential to transform and drive you forward.

Another important source for *Solo for Two* were the writings of the Brazilian author Clarice Lispector. Jean identified with Lispector, a Ukrainian-Jewish immigrant who established herself as a novelist writing in a foreign tongue, Portuguese, and who would become a major voice of twentieth-century literature. Lispector's novels often address the dichotomy of life and death. Her final novel *The Hour of the Star* (1977), which was published posthumously, tells the tragic story of the anti-hero Macabéa, who dies in a car accident after a fortune teller gets her fate mixed up with that of another client. Jean found many references to the themes he was exploring in *The Hour of the Star*. Clarice Lispector also features prominently in the writings of Hélène Cixous. In *The Author in Truth*, Cixous reflects on *The Hour of the Star*: 'How do we behave with the other in the major experiences of life—experiences of separation, experiences, in love, of possession and dispossession, of incorporation and nonincorporation; experiences of mourning by allusion, of real mourning?'[9]

*Solo for Two* begins with a little robot (whom we nicknamed Macheba) projecting waves of light onto the rear wall of the stage. It then moves around the space, dissecting it with a searchlight until it discovers the bodies of two dancers who are standing close together. During the opening duet, the male dancer lifts the female dancer and carries her around. As she gains more and more agency, her body seems to become heavier, eventually pushing her partner down to the floor. The duet isn't about gender but about how our past and our origins sometimes threaten to push us down. Later in the piece, toward the end of his solo, Jean confides in the robot, reciting the opening lines of Lispector's novel in a mix of English and Portuguese. For him as a migrant, the words perfectly summarize his experience that before every beginning, there is another beginning:

> Everything in the world began with a yes. One molecule said yes to another molecule and life was born. But before prehistory there was the prehistory of prehistory and there was the never and there was the yes. It was ever so. I do not know why, but I do know that the universe never began.[10]

Two solos form the backbone of *Solo for Two*. They are presented back-to-back. Most of the movement ideas for them were developed and defined during the first week of research that Jean and I spent in the studio. It became clear that the theme of loss and the succession of endings and beginnings could be best embodied and visualized in the vertical plane. Jean created a solo in which

he slowly peels himself off the floor and struggles through a series of attempts and failures at coming to an upright position. The attempts include many inversions and headstands, which he performs without the support of his arms. They are punctuated by returns to the stillness of his original position, lying on the floor in a corpse pose. Later in the process, we decided to set the second part of this solo to one of Katerina Zakka's traditional *moirolói*, recorded by the British singer and voice coach Cathryn Robson. In the *moirolói* a mother accidentally steps on a stone and discovers it is the tomb of her dead son. In deep pain, she mourns his death. Jean recognized his mother's grief for his brother in this lament. It became an important source of emotion for the creation of his solo.

> Oh, yes yesterday, late at night
> Yesterday my son, I sle—oh—slept
> Up high my son on a stone
> Oh, and look at the tomb my son
> I am crying, oh *kleftiko*
> Buried my stout-hearted son
> Oh, I did not see it, I am unlucky and stepped on it
> Up high my son in my head
> Oh, I hear a sigh my son, a heavy one
> I am sorry my son[11]

As the title of the piece, *Solo for Two*, suggests, Jean knew early on in the creation process that he was looking for a female alter ego who could explore the themes of the piece in a completely different choreographic language. He initially collaborated with the Danish dancer and choreographer Camilla Brogaard, whose approach to the subject matter was much more conceptual and deconstructed. In her original solo, she re-enacts a series of beginnings and endings, such as crashing into the floor or back wall, or slowly withering like a dying tree.

> This is beginning number eight. It is my favorite beginning. End of beginning number eight. It is great to have so many different beginnings. Again. Even if it is hard to choose. Really frustrating. Beginning number eight, again. I love this beginning. This could be the beginning of something. New. Reverse beginning number eight. I wish I also could reverse endings. Sometimes.[12]

Due to funding issues, the creation process of *Solo for Two* had to be suspended several times and became spread out over a period of almost two years. As a result, Camilla was no longer available to participate in the next stage of rehearsals and had to be replaced. The Portuguese dancer and choreographer Maria Fonseca stepped in. She had to make the solo her own, keeping the core structure alive but also adding her own experiences of loss and the attendant emotional charges. In the end, this process of adaptation and re-appropriation was repeated three more times: Margarida Macieira from Portugal and Luna Cenere from Italy both rehearsed the role, while Rita Carpinteiro, also from Portugal, finally embodied it in performance. Each time, Jean had to let go of his partner and alter ego while his body literally adjusted to a new reality. As such, the creation process of *Solo for Two* resembled and even repeated some of the experiences it was referring to, adding to the emotional depth of the final result.

The little robot, Macheba, continues to transform throughout the entire piece. After embodying a search light at the beginning of the piece and during Jean's solo, she becomes an old gramophone or music box that plays fragments of old records, such as the operatic lament 'Una furtiva lagrima,' which is also mentioned in *The Hour of the Star*:

> Una furtiva lagrima' had been the only really beautiful thing in Macabéa's life. Drying her tears, she tried to sing what she heard. ... When she heard her own voice, she began to weep. She was weeping for the first time and had never imagined that there was so much water in her eyes.[13]

At the end of the second solo, both dancers come together again and present a de-constructed 'making of' version of the opening duet, which then transforms into a series of accelerating falls and rebounds that continue until the two dancers have found a common rhythm. The little robot joins again, this time with more agency. First it projects a line into the space that separates the two dancers but still allows them to mirror each other and come together in their breathing. Macheba then introduces a new rhythm, which is picked up by the dancers' bodies. Bending over, they go into a more uplifting jumping sequence reminiscent of Brazilian carnival parades. As the light fades out, the robot takes over one more time, projecting black-and-white pixels onto the bodies, giving them a ghost-like quality. It then projects black-and-white Eadweard Muybridge-like moving images into the space of the stage and above the audience. Macheba acts as camera obscura and as memory box, storing all the experiences and memories up to the present moment.

After our successful collaboration on *Solo for Two*, Jean and I decided that there was still a lot to discover. We continued to research the physical language of laments and began working on a new piece for three women, *As They Are, Mantras for the Body*. Again, the creation process had to be spread over a longer period and is in fact still ongoing. During the ImPulsTanz festival in Vienna in 2019, we organized an initial 'field research' project, during which we delved into the repetitive and cyclical aspects of the laments, exploring their relentless wave-like sensations. Jean developed a physical language that expresses this relentlessness of grieving, while at the same time trying to find ways of letting go.

We invited the Sicilian actress and singer Irene Coticchio to join us and teach Corsican and Sicilian polyphonic laments to the group of participants. Irene is part of the Cowbirds, a group of female performers who have been re-appropriating these songs for female voices. In most ancient traditions, it was the women who took care of the dead and performed the laments. But as these pre-Christian rituals were appropriated by the Church and incorporated into Christian liturgy, men took over. Today, almost all Corsican and Sicilian polyphonic music is primarily sung by men. Irene guided the group in learning the Corsican song *U ricusatu*.

> Today, I find myself all alone,
> Abandoned by people
> I want on this paper
> To write my past
> With the support of the Muse
> As a poor refused one[14]

There are three distinctive voices in Corsican polyphonic songs: the leading voice or *secundo*, which creates the narrative; the *bass*, which provides a deep, sonic layer; and the *tertio*, which embellishes the melody with ornamentations and allows the voice and the energy of the song to spiral upwards. Jean was particularly interested in how this triadic structure could be translated from a vocal into a choreographic concept. In response, the dancers developed their own individual pulse in the vertical dimension by alternating falls and rebounds, while also connecting and supporting each other in the horizontal plane.

Michael S. Schneider's *A Beginner's Guide to Constructing the Universe: The Mathematical Archetypes of Nature, Art, and Science* (1994) has been a great source of inspiration for many of the choreographic processes that I have been involved in. In ten chapters, Schneider discusses the symbolic, spiritual, and secular (i.e., the natural, scientific, and artistic) significance of the numbers one to ten. About the triad and the number three, Schneider writes: 'It gives us the ability to transcend polar bounds and realize the unlimited.'[15] He calls it a threshold that represents rebirth and transformation, reminding his readers that many rituals repeat things three times in order 'to make it whole and bring it to manifestation and completion.'[16] Coming third after the point and the line, the triangle represents 'the birth of structure and surface'[17] and is used in architecture to create self-supporting structures: 'The more triangles, the more weight it will support.'[18] Arguably this applies not only to physics but also to psychology, and in dance too the number three is often considered an important principle.

As Jean and I were working on the piece, Schneider's discussion of the number three reminded us of Merce Cunningham's statement that choreography only starts with three bodies in space. In Indian classical dance there is the ti-ha principle, according to which every movement has to be repeated at least three times: the first time to introduce it, the second time to remember and recognize it, and the third time to enjoy it. Jean had also been reading about the symbolism of the number three in Buddhism: the Three Refuges (also called the Three Jewels or Triple Gem), the Three Realms (or *Triloka*), and the Three Bodies (or *Trikaya*). Finally, and in hindsight, we realized that if one included the robot Macheba in the cast, our previous piece *Solo for Two* had in fact been a trio.

After the workshop at ImPulsTanz, Jean invited the three performers to a residency in London to begin the next stage of the research process. Camilla Brogaard and Margarida Macieira, who had both been involved in the creation process of *Solo for Two*, were joined by the Brazilian-Palestinian dancer and choreographer Rafaela Sahyoun. Jean wanted to explore the power of being vulnerable and embodying one's emotions. 'I want to create a fearlessness, a sense of offering the body to the space, proposing to the collective

body no place to hide, a willingness to be vulnerable, to share, to hear and to let go.'[19] Highlighting vulnerability as a source of female power had a political dimension. The traditional laments were not only a way of expressing and eventually letting go of pain—they also frequently became a protest against patriarchy. As a male choreographer, Jean was questioning his own role in relation to his female performers. He wanted to give them as much agency as possible, not only during the creation process, but also in future performances. Together they decided to work with a scored improvisation practice, which resembles the performance practice of the traditional laments. The lamenters use past somatic and emotional memories to weave a new version of the lament in the here and now. Together with Camilla, Margarida, and Rafaela, Jean continued to research different ways in which their three bodies could relate to each other. Through entanglement and disentanglement, they created a variety of different sculptural clusters of three. A first public showing was organized at the October Gallery in London on the invitation of Kathelin Gray, who curated a larger event around it entitled *Presence/Absence/Presence*.

The work-in-progress showing starts with the three dancers in a motionless position—one lying, one sitting and one standing—while the space around them changes color and focus through strips of LED lights that are lighting up at different times. Slowly, the constellation of the three bodies transforms both in the vertical and the horizontal plane. Relationships are redefined through small shifts in proximity. By changing the pulse and the rhythm of her movements, each dancer can leave the triadic support structure to develop a solo, returning to the structure when she has finished. Together they accelerate, keeping moments of stillness as punctuation. They start walking in circular patterns, constantly changing the central points to determine where they will meet or cross each other. Out of the circular patterns a new, shared pulse emerges, which is articulated in the upper body and the chest. This is also the part of the body where we store our grief.

> I want to develop with the dancers a movement practice that combines polycentric continuous motion qualities and repetitive pulsations; to find the relationship between these two qualities in the dynamic rhythms shifts between them, both in the individual and as a group; to research and find principles that we agree on collectively, that we can

research, repeat and apply every time in a practice based
on listening to each other and to the space.[20]

Eventually, the dancers come together in a sitting position. They
touch for the first time. The pulse slows down and they further
entangle into a 'clam,' gently rocking and cradling each other. On
the soundtrack you hear them tuning in to each other during one of
their voice practice rehearsals. Out of this intimacy and proximity,
the Corsican lament, *U lamentu di Ghjesu* emerges.

> Oh you sleeping
> inside this stone grave
> for having suffered
> so many injuries and wounds
> the atrocious torture
> that finally made you die too
> now you can rest, quiet, still
> you do not suffer any more[21]

While working with Jean on *Solo for Two*, I had traveled to London
to see the installation *An Occupation of Loss* by the American visual
artist Taryn Simon. Simon had originally created *An Occupation of
Loss* in New York with the architect Shohei Shigematsu, building a
monumental installation of eleven concrete towers resembling the
pipes of an organ. All the towers were chapels in which professional
lamenters from all over the world practiced their living traditions.
They included lamenters from Albania, Azerbaijan, Bhutan, Burkina
Faso, Cambodia, China, Colombia, Ecuador, Ghana, Greece, India,
Kenya, Kyrgyzstan, Malaysia, Romania, Russia, and Venezuela:

> In *An Occupation of Loss*, professional mourners simulta-
> neously broadcast their lamentations, enacting rituals of
> grief. Their sonic mourning is performed in recitations that
> include northern Albanian laments, which seek to excavate
> 'uncried words'; Wayuu laments, which safeguard the soul's
> passage to the Milky Way; Greek Epirotic laments, which
> bind the story of a life with its afterlife; and Yezidi laments,
> which map a topography of displacement and exile.[22]

The official catalogue of the project[23] includes a conversation
between Homi K. Bhabha and Taryn Simon, in which they

discuss how the project relates to the here and now of the political situation in the USA, with its incidents of war, terrorist attacks, mass shootings, and the Black Lives Matter movement. Referencing Bhabha, Simon defines the space that the professional lamenters occupy as a 'third space that opens up—a space that is neither reality nor fiction, a space that is maybe both at the same time.'[24] Simon and Bhabha also agree that the 'artifice' of the professional lamenters is a necessary condition for the emotional impact they have on their audiences:

> And the artifice of mourning—whether it is embodied in photography, performance, sculpture, or poetry—intensifies the affective capability of communication because it is more than simply a subjective 'expression' of an idea or an emotion: it is an act of transference, a process of translation that moves between the work and the viewer.[25]

In London, Simon recreated the installation in an abandoned underground car park in Islington, going back to her original architectural source of inspiration: the structure resembled a well, with all of its symbolism and its specific sonic qualities. She used the existing concrete vaults that circled down several floors and only added small concrete shrines in which the lamenters took their places. Entering into this world really felt like a descent into the underworld. At the beginning of the journey, the lamenters entered the space in a procession from the bottom of the concrete pit. The audience were then invited to descend further into the concrete labyrinth, where they would stumble on shrines at random, free to decide for themselves if they wanted to keep exploring or stay for a while to listen more closely to one particular tradition of laments. It was my luck to be immediately drawn to the Greek shrine: Nota Kaltsouni, Vangelis Kotsos and Nikos Menoudakis had brought their tight-knit versions of the polyphonic laments of Epirus.

> There exists a strict hierarchy among the group of lamenters: the leading singer as a narrator, the one who 'knits' the lament; the singer, called 'birdie,' who improvises and often uses bird-like sounds; and finally, one or more singers who keep the straight, smooth level of the melody.[26]

Experiencing the diversity of these songs of mourning in this well-thought-out architectural environment was powerful, but at the same time there was a troubling commercial aspect to the entire project. As a contemporary artwork, the London edition was commissioned by Artangel, which had created a successful media campaign around it. As a result, the audience had to be staggered and divided into shifts, enabling several large groups of people to attend per evening. Those lucky enough to get tickets had to queue up at the entrance and were then chased through the experience in less than an hour, only to be ushered out through a fire exit to make room for the next crowd waiting to enter. The artistic consumerism that accompanied the event left little room for intimacy. There had been a great potential for emotionality, but the experience made me realize that I needed to remain vigilant and careful about how I used the laments in the projects that I was accompanying as a dramaturg.

As we left, we all received the catalogue for the installation. It did not contain the usual explanatory artistic notes, but instead documented the tedious visa application processes that the artist had to go through to invite all the different singers first to New York and now also to London. In the US, Simon had to apply for a P-3 visa ('Artist or entertainer coming to be part of a culturally unique program'), which involved piles of expert testimonials validating each performer as 'culturally unique.' In the UK, she had to apply for Tier 5 (Creative and Sporting) visas. She was asked to prove to the immigration authorities that each applicant had an 'attribute which would be unlikely to be available in the EEA labour force, e.g., a certain physical appearance, physical talent or linguistic or vocal skill.' The supporting documents for the American visa application[27] of the Greek lamenters from Epirus state: 'Each group's polyphonic laments are unique because the members of each group are related to each other and have shared life experiences that bond them and influence the subjects of their laments.'[28] As more and more borders are closing, also for artists, the documentation of the visa application process added an important political dimension to the project. 'Simon documents the routes of the application process to reveal the underlying structures governing global exchange, the movement of bodies, and the hierarchies of art and culture.'[29]

Similar to the political aspect of Simon's project in relation to contemporary issues of migration, others have used the lament form within a post-colonial discourse, when people have died away

from home 'uncried' or when parts of the own culture got forbidden and lost under pressure of the colonial regime. While I was working on the first draft of this book during my time as a fellow of the International Research Center 'Interweaving Performance Cultures' at the Freie Universität in Berlin, HAU Hebbel am Ufer presented the project *Return to Sender* (2015). Its aim was to address German and European colonial history, symbolically 'reversing' the dynamics of the 1884 Conference of Berlin, in which the European colonial powers divided up Africa among each other. As part of the project, the Congolese choreographer Faustin Linyekula performed *Statue of Loss*, a dance solo set to live music. The piece is a lament for and dialogue with the Congolese soldiers who fought and died in World War I, both in Africa and in Europe. In his choreographic work Linyekula frequently embarks on a 'dialogue with history,' uncovering parts of our shared colonial history that have been forgotten or remain unacknowledged in the West. He recounts how he visited an exhibition in Brussels on World War I, only to see that Africa had been left out entirely from its account of this historical period. In the 1920s, the Congolese veteran Paul Panda Farnana proposed a plan to build a monument for the unknown soldiers who died, at the mouth of the Congo river. But Farnana died before he could realize his plan and the anonymous soldiers remained 'uncried.' Linyekula's danced lament is a response to this absence, and an answer to the question he asked himself when he was starting out on the work: 'What acknowledgement has been made of their sacrifice and what's left apart from the ghost of a monument that was never built?'[30] As part of the process of creating the solo, he searched for the names of individual soldiers in the sparse surviving records, in order to be able to personally address them as he mourned their deaths. In a talk that Linyekula gave at the institute, he described how his heritage is 'a pile of ruins,' not only materially but also mentally. He said that art is a form of activism that involves revisiting these ruins to build temporary shelters as part of an 'aesthetics of survival.'[31]

In 2017, I was invited by Yana Meerzon of the Studies in Migration Research Group of the University of Ottawa to give my workshop on writing one's own laments. One of the participants was Vivi Sørensen, an Inuk actress, theater director, playwright, and traditional drum and mask dancer from Nuuk, Greenland. She responded with a lament for the disappearance of the drum in her culture, which had come under colonial and religious pressure. In West Greenland, where German and Danish colonizers replaced the local music culture with their own religious hymns, the drum became illegal. Local drum songs completely disappeared from living practice, only surviving as narratives in stories and myths. The people lost all memory of how it looked and what it sounded like.[32]

In the 1970s, the Norwegian actor Reidar Nilsson, a former student of Odin Teatret, created Tuukkaq Theater in Denmark, where many Greenlandic artists have studied. These Greenlanders researched and revived Greenlandic performance practices. Some of Tuukkaq Theatre's members returned to Greenland in the 1980s to create their own theater company, Silamiut Theater, which became the National Theatre of Greenland in 2011. Vivi took part in drama classes at Silamiut as a teenager and eventually learnt how to drum dance by attending workshops and learning from Thomasine Umerinneq, an elder in Tasiilaq, East Greenland. When she learnt the different rhythms of the surviving drum cultures of the other regions, she started to recognize the silenced drum rhythms in some of the traditional songs from her own region, particularly in one type of a capella mourning song, *Inuggooq*. In one of these mourning songs, *Qatserlini*, she began to hear how the silenced drum rhythms could be reactivated.

My drum.
I remember being a teenager and writing about my missing identity and saying to you, my drum, where are you?
My drum.
Some time between 1721 and the early 1900s you disappeared.
So severely satanic and so illegal that we in the West of Greenland don't even know how you looked like, how you smelled like, how you sounded like.
My drum.
Taken away. Made illegal. Made shameful. Mute. But the heart beat was still beating. ...
Where were you?
At last I found you. ...
If you listen carefully, you're there in some songs.
My people kept you.
The beating of the drum might have disappeared but some

songs were still there.
One song in particular stands out.
A wailing song. A song about loss.
A song sung by a woman whose brother had gone hunting in his qajaq on the most still waters and yet the walrus managed to break his qajaq and crack his body.
If one listens carefully in this one song one can hear the drum beat.[33]

When I gave my workshop in Ottawa, I also met the visual artist Laura Taler, who contacted me afterwards to tell me that she had recognized part of her own work in the laments we shared. In Laura's recent work, she thematizes autobiographical experiences of migration and uses forms of laments to express these. Laura is an interdisciplinary artist who intertwines performance, film, and the visual arts. Reflecting on her artistic journey, from choreography to dance-films, to visual arts projects, Laura explains that her experience of moving through six different languages as a child resulted in her being more comfortable in communicating through movements, gestures, and facial expressions rather than through words.

I was born in Romania, where I went to a German Kindergarten, I moved to Italy where I went to Hebrew school and then settled in bilingual Canada. Most of the time I was not able to understand what people were saying to me so I had to rely on my ability to read, mimic and reintegrate the gestures and facial expressions of others through my own body.[34]

This is a common practice that all children use to some extent in order to understand each other, especially on an affective level: they mimic and embody each other. Laura translated these experiences into her artistic practice by consciously exploring the motif of the doppelgänger. 'I chose to perform as my doppelgänger, understanding that this character would give me a measure of distance to address concerns that were perhaps too difficult to address as myself.'[35]

In her most recent work, the video triptych *THREE SONGS*, Laura explicitly references the lament form. *THREE SONGS* consists of three separate but related video installations on multiple channels. Just like the Greek *moirológhia* are always strongly embedded in a particular landscape, Laura's doppelgänger in each of the videos sings a song resembling a lament while being embedded in a particular landscape or environment, in a language that is not her own. In *Song #1*, Laura sings the Romanian song *Uite usa as vrea sa mor* (This is how I'd like to die) in a German forest, near the Baltic sea. In *Song #2* she revisits the landscape and buildings on her grandmother's farm in Romania for the first time in twenty years, singing the Argentinian tango song *El adiós* (The Goodbye). *Song #3* is a split-screen video in which she sings the Yiddish song *Rumania, Rumania, Rumania: Geven Amul a Land a Zise, a Sheyne* (Romania, Romania, Romania: Once there was a land, sweet and lovely).

In *Song #2*, Laura temporarily embodies her grandmother through a costume that helps her fit into the village landscape. The disguise is an act of artifice that is only revealed half-way through the video, when she takes off her wig, rubs her short-cropped hair and puts the wig back on in one simple, smooth gesture. This uncanny gesture is performed through a simple editing technique that reverses the timeline and jolts the viewer by literally saying 'this is not real.' The latter fits with something Leader writes in *The New Black*: 'mourning thus involves a certain making artificial.'[36] In many cultures, mourning rituals reverse established conventions or roles to highlight the liminal state in which the mourner dwells. My own understanding of the *moirológhia* is that artifice is also necessary to 'perform' the mourning: the emotions of grief have to be re-embodied and renegotiated with a proper balance of control and loss of control, distance and proximity, for them to become integrated and resolved.

A similar sense of artifice is achieved by mixing language and non-language, stylized cries and sobs which often support the affect of the vocalizations. In one of her earlier video works, *cry* (2009), Laura slows down the footage of a baby crying, until the sound's pitch convincingly sounds like the sobs of a grown man. The discrepancy between image and sound is both comical and disturbing. In *THREE SONGS*, Laura deliberately decides to embrace 'the foreign.' She chooses to sing—'a performative technique that is foreign to her'—in languages that she hasn't mastered perfectly, such as the Argentinian tango song. In her personal notes on the creation process of *Song #2*, she writes:

The video installation of *Song #2* consists of five video channels of different lengths. In the first channel, Laura sings the song while sitting at her grandmother's kitchen table, re-enacting everyday tasks such as pulling back a curtain or folding blankets. These actions are rhythmically interspersed with stills of the house's interior, close-ups of her face, and close-ups of the textures of the objects she is manipulating. The channel ends with a series of wide shots of Laura moving through the vast, empty fields around the farm. In the second channel, she performs a series of dance steps resembling traditional folk dances and *mudra*-like hand gestures in her grandmother's bedroom. Again, the camera moves between wide shots and close-ups, between movement and stillness. In the third channel, her grandmother's neighbors sit on benches outside the house, witnessing and commenting on her endeavor as an audience would. The power of living traditions such as the Greek *moirológhia* is that they allow for the individual mourning to be performed in front of a larger community, so that the emotions can be shared in a dramatized ethics of care. In the fourth channel, we see the farm complex from a bird's eye view, with Laura walking through it. The fifth channel simply shows the song lyrics, translated in English and French, scrolling down the screen:

As time has passed
You always lived in me
And these fields that saw us
Together smiling
Wonder if oblivion
Has cured me of you
And among the winds
My complaints go

Dying in echoes
Looking for you
While far away
Other arms and other kisses
Imprison you and tell me
You will never return[38]

Finally, in *Song #3*, Laura further amplifies the theme of the doppelgänger, both thematically and formally. In the split-screen video we see her embody a Yiddish singing cabaret artist in a Berlin night club of the 1930s while also working (as herself) on a Janus bust in the ateliers and storage rooms of the *Gipsformerei* in Berlin. For more than 200 years, this plaster cast replica workshop has created high-quality replicas of sculptures and art works from the collections of the Staatliche Museen, Berlin, but also from other European museums. Its store contains more than 7000 plaster casts. Performing as her doppelgänger and an employee at the *Gipsformerei*, Laura surreptitiously inserts her two-headed self-portrait bust onto the shelves among all the historical busts, ostensibly inserting her own self and history into a workshop that is all about repeating and paying respect to the past.

Laura Taler's *THREE SONGS* is a contemporary lament in which she uses her experiences as a migrant to revisit the landscapes and memories of her past. As a 'foreigner' in different languages and different artistic mediums, she performs and shares her mourning in order to trans-form. The experience of the migrant resembles the transformative process of mourning, in which one has to re-member and renegotiate one's past memories of places, people and languages in order to start anew.

# Notes

1   Traditional *moirolói*:
    ενιτεμένο μου πουλί
    Και παραπονεμένο
    μωρέ ξένε μου
    Η ξενιτιά σε χαίρεται
    Κι εγώ ’χω τον καημό σου
    Τι να σου στείλω, ξένε μου
    Αυτού στα ξένα που ’σαι
    Να στείλω μήλο σέπεται
    Τριαντάφυλλο μαραίνει
    Σου στέλλω και το δάκρυ μου
    Σ’ ένα χρυσό μαντίλι
    Τα δάκρυ μ’ ήταν καυτερό
    Και καίηται το μαντίλι.
2   Danforth 1982, p. 90.
3   Kotsos in Simon 2017, p. 202.
4   Danforth 1982, p. 173.
5   Ibid., p. 173.
6   Traditional *moirolói*, transcription and translation Xanthoula Dakouvano:
    Αχ τώρα στα ξεχωρίσματα ελα
    γιέ μου να φιληθούμε,αχ, ελα
    γιέ μου να φιληθούμε,
    ωρ›γιατί έχουμε ζωή και θάνατο,
    ποιος ξέρει αν ανταμωθούμε
    αχ, ποιος ξέρει αν ανταμωθούμε.
    Έλα έλα που σου λέω, μη με
    τυρανάς και κλαίω
    Άχ αλλού εσύ, αλλού εγώ,
    θιαμαίνομαι γιέ μου που ζούμε
    Ω, βόηθα Χριστέ και Παναγιά,
    τα δυό να ξανανταμωθούμε, τα
    δυό να ξανανταμωθούμε
    Ταίρι μου ξενιτεμένο, έλα που
    σε περιμένω
7   *The New York Times*, April 10, 2020.
8   From a personal message by Jean Abreu.
9   Cixous 1991, p. 154.
10  Lispector 1977, 1986, p. 11.
11  Traditional *moirolói*, originally sung by Katerina Zakka, translated by Cathryn Robson and Evangelos Andrikopoulos:
    Ωρέ ναι ψες προψές
    Ψες γιέ μου
    κοιμή-ωρε- κοιμήθηκα
    ψηλά γιε μου σε ενα λιθάρι
    Ωρέ και κοίτα μνήμα γιε μου
    Κλαίω ωρέ κλέφτικο
    Θαμμένο γιε μου παλικάρι
    Ωρέ δεν το είδα, ο μαύρος και
    το πά -ωρε- το πάτησα
    Ψηλά γιε μου μες το κεφάλι
    Ωρέ και ακούω αναστεναγμό γιε μου βαρύ
    Συγγνώμη παλικάρι μου
12  *Solo for Two*, original performance text.
13  Lispector 1977, 1986, p. 50.
14  Traditional Corsican song, transcription and translation, Irene Coticchio:
    Oghje mi trovu sulettu
    Da la ghjente abbandunata
    Vogliu qui sopra à la carta
    Inscrive lu mio passatu
    Cù l’aiuta di la musa
    D’una povara Ricusata
15  Schneider 1994, p. 39.
16  Ibid., p. 43.
17  Ibid., p. 44.
18  Ibid., p. 46.
19  From Jean’s working notes on *As They Are*.
20  Ibid.
21  Traditional Corsican lament *U lamentu di Ghjesu*:
    O tù chì dormi
    in sta petra sculpita
    d’avè suffertu
    da colpi è ferita
    dopu d’atroci martiri
    persu hai ancu la vita,
    oghje riposi tranquillu
    a tò suffrenza hè finite
22  From the program text of *A Matter of Loss*, the London edition.
23  Simon 2017.
24  Ibid., p. 20.
25  Ibid., p. 21.
26  Vantzos in Simon 2017, p. 87.
27  Form I-129, expert letter, March 30, 2016.
28  Simon 2017, p. 87.
29  From the program text of *A Matter of Loss*, the London edition.
30  From the program text for *Statue of Loss*, HAU Hebbel am Ufer, March 14, 2015.
31  From my personal notes from a lecture that Faustin Linyekula gave in Berlin at the International Research Institute ‘Interweaving Performance Cultures,’ March 12, 2015. A transcript of this lecture has been published as Faustin Linkyekula, ‘An Artist/Activist Moving (Across) Borders,’ in Gabriele Brandstetter and Holger Hartung, eds., *Moving (Across) Borders: Performing Translation, Intervention, Participation* (Bielefeld: transcript Verlag, 2017), pp. 135–155.
32  In other regions of Greenland, such as in East and North Greenland, the drum survived because the forced assimilation of the Inuit happened there at a later time.
33  Vivi Sørensen’s lament, original text.
34  Laura Taler, unpublished lecture.
35  Ibid.

36  Leader 2008, p. 105.
37  Laura Taler, unpublished lecture.
38  Argentinian tango song, translation
    Laura Taler:

> Sobre el tiempo transcurrido
> Vives siempre en mi
> Y estos campos que nos vieron
> Juntos sonreir
> Me preguntan si el olvido
> Me curo de ti
> Y entre los vientos
> Se van mis quejas
> Muriendo en ecos
> Buscandote
> Mientras que lejos
> Otros brazos y otros besos
> Te aprisionan y me dicen
> Que ya nunca has de volver

# Lamenting Unlived Lives[1]

Skin Kori (For My Daughter)

> You left me alone, very early, my child
>
> Oh Mother
>
> Everybody will ask for you and look for you
> Oh, my girl, you were so beautiful that you made death jealous
> He took you in spring when everything was blossoming
> You destroyed our family
> You took our happiness
>
> I am not alone here
> There are a lot of other young people[2]

In most of the psychological literature on grief and mourning there is a special place reserved for the specific mourning of parents for their children, which stands out as extremely painful since it is a reversal of the natural order of things. The grief for the unrealized potential of a life not fully lived is often heightened by strong feelings of guilt and anger. When the author Kate Saunders was invited to reflect on C.S. Lewis' *A Grief Observed*, she did so from the perspective of her own mourning for her son Felix: 'My world is dark and will always be dark. The death of a child is a wound that will never heal, and there's no getting used to hefting round that sack of everlasting sorrow.'[3] David Kessler's reflections on the sixth stage of grief, *Finding Meaning*, are very much inspired by his own grief for his adopted son David. He dedicates an entire chapter of his book to 'child loss,' and another more specifically to miscarriages and infant loss. He sums up the sense of injustice that many parents grapple with—'A child is not supposed to die before his or her parents'—and admits: 'I have never met anyone who found a good reason for it. Why would we live in a world where young people die? How cruel is that?'[4] Julia Samuel, in her book *Grief Works*, also writes specifically about parents mourning for their children. She acknowledges that 'guilt is very intense for bereaved parents. More than in any other bereavement, they tend to hold themselves responsible for the death of their child.'[5] Daniel Leader in turn mentions miscarriages as a 'significant example' of a loss that is often not acknowledged by society. 'What is a tragedy for the mother and father may be ignored or denied by others, blocking the designation of the event *as a loss*. Yet there is a vital human need to designate events symbolically.'[6]


> One cannot discuss a dead child, whether miscarried, aborted, stillborn, diseased, or killed, without also activating the archetypal associations with it, which are, by nature, powerful. As had already been explained, the image of the dead child constellates feelings of inadequacy, shame, bodily defect, corruptibility of flesh, lost hope, lost future, and emptiness.[7]

In her book *Mourning Unlived Lives* (1989, 2018), the Jungian analyst Judith A. Savage discusses archetypal patterns of mourning while focusing on infant and childbearing loss. She gives examples of case studies from her psychoanalytic practice which she interweaves with mythical and religious stories and images. Among the myths she references are a legend about Buddhist nuns (*Bhikkunis*) who were bereaved mothers, Demeter's grief for Persephone, and the Christian iconography of the Virgin Mary. Her analysis reveals that 'childbearing losses are mourned not only for what was, but also for what might have been.' Because 'the child is the object of the parents' imaginative projections ... they mourn the child of the imagination, that part of themselves which seems now to have no possibility of embodiment in the world.'[8] She also writes that what makes mourning for an infant or child particularly problematic is 'the incompatibility of the two simultaneously occurring psychological processes of detachment and attachment.'[9] Referencing Ronald J. Knapp's book *Beyond Endurance: When a Child Dies* (1986), she bases her analysis on his list of six 'findings,' or experiences that are common to parents who have lost a child: 1. the vow to never to forget the child, 2. the wish to die, 3. a revitalization of religious beliefs, 4. a change of values, 5. more tolerance, and 6. shadow grief. The lament form is particularly suited to expressing the first experience, 'the vow never to forget,' or need to *re-member*.

In his essay *Re-membering Osiris: From the Death Cult to Cultural Memory* (2000), the Egyptologist Jan Assmann gives a detailed overview of the culture of ancient Egypt's rootedness in the cult of the dead. He explains that this cult focused 'not on the living body in its beauty, strength, and vulnerability, but rather on the body of the deceased and the practice of its symbolic

reanimation.'[10] Assmann describes the myth of Isis as a literal act of re-membering: The Goddess collects the limbs of her dead husband and reassembles them while singing her lament-like songs.

> The motif of the dismemberment and dispersal of body parts, then, does not describe a literal tearing apart of the corpse, but rather interprets the actual lifelessness of the body as a decay of community and the dismemberment of connection.[11]

It follows that every act of re-membering or re-membrance can be understood as a process of de- and reconstructing the original event or experience. In recent research, neuroscientists have discovered that the brain rewrites and even overwrites neurological patterns that are activated by memory. The act of re-membering thus allows the original experience to be transformed. However, in order for this to happen, the remembering needs to be repeated over and over again in a cyclical pattern, until the lost 'members' are finally re-integrated. An overwhelming emotional experience such as the death of a loved one (and the attendant mourning process) will require many cycles of re-membering, both by the individual mourners and their larger family networks, which are often forced into new constellations by the sudden absence of the deceased.

The last experience in Knapp's list, 'shadow grief,' is exacerbated by the taboos surrounding infant mourning in our society. Mourning processes are frequently not properly expressed and linger in the shadows. They are also commonly accompanied by emotions of anger and a sense of injustice at the order of events. These feelings of rage are then often projected onto oneself or onto others, such as for example the medical staff who cared for the sick child, other children, or one's partner. 'The projection of anger is, of course, a psychological defense, a warding off, and is normal to all grief.'[12] In a couple, this anger is not only about blaming each other for the child's death, but also about not understanding the uniqueness of each other's grief and mourning processes. As a result, many relationships break down following the loss of a child. Parents are unable to share their mourning. Both Kessler and Samuel give detailed descriptions of relationships and marriages breaking down in such circumstances. 'I think they end because of how the parents judge each other for not sharing the same feelings they have and not expressing them in the same way.'[13]

Lars von Trier's film *Antichrist* (2009) must be one of the most violent and controversial depictions of how grief for a child is experienced differently by the parents, leading to a violent breakup of the couple. *Antichrist* starts with a prologue in which a toddler falls to his death from a bedroom window while his parents are having sex. The mother (Charlotte Gainsbourg) experiences deep grief, which the father (Willem Dafoe), who is a psychiatrist, tries to treat. They retreat to a forest, where their relationship becomes more and more violent. Both are visited by supernatural visions and nightmares, which include images of witches being persecuted. When I saw Von Trier's film shortly after it was released, I had strong feelings of déjà-vu and was reminded of my own mourning process. In order to come to terms with my original grief and the unlived mourning for my father's death, I, like the couple in the film, needed to be alone for a while. Among other things, this period of solitude led to the end of my first marriage. It also allowed me to take the time and space I needed to cyclically renegotiate my original unexpressed mourning without continuing to affect my sons. In the opening chapter of this book, I mentioned that it was the end of a new love relationship that made me literally re-live the original shock of grief for my father, almost exactly 29 years after he died. The experience liquefied my sadness into tears and was the starting point for rebalancing the energy in my body that had been fueled by too much suppressed anger. Shortly afterwards, I was invited to Greece for the first time, where I discovered the *moirológhia* and started on the artistic journey of researching and applying the lament form.

But life had more experiences in store for me. My second intense love relationship after my divorce was with a Canadian woman of Greek origin. When we met, our personal histories with each other's cultures were part of the attraction. After a long-distance courtship, during which we would meet occasionally in Canada, Belgium, or Greece and exchanged long, hand-written letters detailing our feelings and our pasts, I decided to move to Canada.[14] We were both in our early forties and engaged in a passionate relationship that was complicated by us not having fully come to terms with issues from our pasts. At one point, I had to return to Europe in order to participate in the creation process of *zero degrees*. While I was away, we learnt that she was pregnant. The news was particularly surprising because she had been told that she would not be able to have children due to a medical condition. When her doctors confirmed the pregnancy, they said that because of her medical history, the chances of a miscarriage would be very high. This caused great anxiety, which, combined with the physical distance between us, put extra pressure on an already fragile relationship.

When the miscarriage did happen, early on in the pregnancy, before I was able to return, it also ended our relationship in an abrupt and violent manner. How do you mourn an unborn child? How do you bridge the difference between the mourning of the mother, who experiences the loss at a deep somatic level, and the father, for whom it necessarily remains a 'virtual reality'? And how do the mourning processes of both parents affect all the other family members, even those who are yet to be born?

The latter question is the topic of *The White Book* (2017) by the South Korean author Han Kang. In Confucian philosophy, white is the color of mourning. Kang's book is a re-membering of her older sister, whom she never met because she died hours after being born prematurely. 'My mother's first child died, I was told, less than two hours into life. I was told that she was a girl, with a face as white as a crescent-moon rice cake.'[15] The grief and mourning of a parent or sibling for a child is particularly painful since it involves grieving a life that has not yet achieved its full potential. This is true no matter what age the child is when it dies, whether it is a few years or a few hours old, or not even born. The act of remembering and performing mourning becomes an act of imagination, of conjuring 'what-ifs.' In Kang's case, who wrote the book while living in Warsaw, the imagined life of her unknown sister begins to resemble the city, which was completely destroyed at the end of World War II. 'And I think of her coming here instead of me. To this curiously familiar city, whose death and life resemble her own.'[16] Is it a coincidence that the individual tragedy of a child's death is associated with the equally extreme collective tragedies of genocide in both Kang's and Forest's books, as well as in Von Trier's film?

There are many other deaths that are remembered and mourned in *The White Book*: a father who dies in a mountaineering accident; a dog named Fog; a brother and sister who enshrine the bones of their mother in an ossuary and later burn a white cotton robe in her memory; two university classmates who both die in accidents in short succession and for whom two trees are planted on campus; an uncle who dies of an alcohol addiction; all the dead in

Warsaw and South-Korea's histories who have 'been insufficiently mourned';[17] and Kang's own future death.

Kang identifies with her sister. She looks at the world through her sister's eyes, enumerating all the 'if onlys' that her mother used to recite: 'What it would be like if I'd had an older sister.'[18] *The White Book* is structured similarly to Roland Barthes's book about his grief for his mother, consisting of short passages and memories, often only one page long, separated by blank pages and an occasional black-and-white photograph. The emptiness of the blank pages punctuates the reading flow and creates a distinctive rhythm: absence, presence, absence.

In 2018, I was part of an international jury that awarded the first prize of the Czech Dance Platform Awards to the solo performance *The Narrator* by Spitfire Company. *The Narrator* is a collaboration between Spitfire's director Petr Boháč and the piece's solo performer, the French-Portuguese dancer Cécile Da Costa. When the audience enters the space, Cécile is already on stage—a raised, square, wooden floor surrounded by large glass boxes, which are filled with different materials: bricks, sand, gravel, and water. Cécile begins by taking red bricks out of one of the boxes, one by one, dusting them off and carefully placing them one on top of another. At one point she starts to dance a stylized, deconstructed flamenco routine, which she immediately interrupts to pick up the last two bricks. She holds one in each hand and stretches her arms out in front of her, creating a visible strain in her body. She addresses the audience: 'I am counting the empty chairs: 1, 2, 3, 4, 5. I am counting the French people. I am counting the broken bricks. I am counting until someone stops me.' Between each series of counts she breathes in and out, lowering and raising her arms which are weighed down by the bricks. Her tone is light and the audience laughs along with her, but this changes abruptly when she issues her final statement: 'I am counting my unborn children: 1, 2, 3.'[19]

Throughout the hour-long solo there are sharp disruptions in the mood and energy of the piece—a discontinuity that is typical for any mourning process. Cécile is accompanied live by the musician Jan Šikl, who alternates between energetic, percussive rhythms on his drum set and eerie, haunting melodies on his saxophone. A first movement section, in which Cécile slowly and deliberately brings the bricks together and separates them again, ends with her throwing them into one of the glass boxes, which is

filled with a kind of gravel. She then jumps into the box, picks up some of the gravel and starts a repetitive, mantra-like recitation in different languages:

> These empty chairs are not the name of God. This performance is not the name of God ... My silence is not the name of God. My shoulders, my belly are not the name of God. My desire is not the name of God. My sex is not the name of God. My love is not the name of God.[20]

The recitation, which gradually transforms into a powerful, distorted wailing, is a reference to another source of inspiration for *The Narrator*, the novel *Syngué Sabour, Pierre de Patience* (*The Patience Stone*, 2008) by the French-Afghan writer Atiq Rahimi. In it, Rahimi tells the story of an Afghan woman who sits by the side of her husband, a soldier, who is wounded and in a coma. While she takes care of him, she talks to him and confesses some of her female experiences in a male-dominated world. Cécile's solo creates invisible threads linking her own story to that of other women.

There is a short pause, during which she readjusts some of the moveable stage lights, before jumping into another glass box, which is filled with sand. She sings the first line of a soothing Portuguese song, almost a lullaby. She then steps back onto the stage, whispering the same line over and over again: 'I have to remember that I have to forget everything.'[21] The next movement sequence intertwines flamenco steps with martial-art-inspired gestures. Music and movement escalate again into a percussive staccato dialogue, during which Cécile destroys the tower of bricks with a hammer. She picks up one of the broken bricks and tapes it to her hand—another weight she has to carry during the next part of the performance.

The high-energy performance has a relentless forward drive, lurching from internalized to externalized, physical rage. Only the fragments of the Portuguese song offer brief moments of relief. Cécile enters another glass box, this one filled with water. She gets out and re-enters the box with the sand. She throws the stones back into their box and eventually begins to dismantle the wooden boards of the main stage, using them to shut the glass boxes. Turning them around, she reveals a mirrored surface and creates a wall. Exhausted, she counts one more time: 1, 2, 3. She sings another verse of her lullaby/lament for her unborn children. The relentless deconstruction and reconstruction of the performance space ends with her trembling and shaking in front of the mirror wall: 'I forget you. Still in my belly, in my heart ... This night, I dreamt of water. An immense cold ... You won't suffer. You have never suffered. You will never suffer ... You hear me.'[22]

When my partner and I were both living through the experience of her miscarriage, separated and at a distance, I found Jan Chozen Bays' book *Jizo Bodhisattva: Guardian of Children, Travelers, and Other Voyagers* (2003) in a second-hand bookstore. The book charts the history of the Buddhist bodhisattva or saint Jizo and describes a ritual practice that developed in post-war Japan and more recently also in the US, called Mizuko Jizo or water-baby ceremony, it is a way of remembering and honoring children who have died, in particular those who were lost through miscarriage or abortion.

> Both the Mizuko Jizo and the mizuko ceremony arose in Japan in the 1960s in response to a human need, to relieve the suffering emerging from the experience of the large number of women who had undergone abortions after World War II.[23]

Reading about this practice, I felt the need to have my own private ritual to commemorate and lament the child's 'unlived' life, and also to make space for grieving the violent break-up that had resulted from it. Every year on the anniversary of the miscarriage, I would take a small object that was particularly meaningful and valuable to me, for instance a silver coin I had inherited from my father, and wrap it as if it were a precious gift. I would then take the package to the closest river and throw it in, meditating on this 'unlived' life while I walked to and from the river. I kept doing this for almost ten years, visiting rivers in Montreal, London, Antwerp, Amsterdam, and Vienna.

This small personal ritual, which was inspired by reading a book on Buddhist practices, is a good example of what Meredith B. McGuire calls 'lived religion.' In her book *Lived Religion: Faith and Practice in Everyday Life* (2008), she describes it as a practice that is characterized by eclecticism and a blending of different traditions. Rather than being connected to a single faith, it consists of a series of personal rituals that in our contemporary world are often borrowed from a diversity of traditions. She argues that every

lived religious practice blends the material and the spiritual and often has an embodied experience at its core. 'People use objects and their own bodies in popular religious practices that celebrate and remember the sacred-within-the-profane.'[24] The rituals commemorating the dead are an important part of this. McGuire gives the example of the Mexican *descansos* (resting places), roadside shrines that are created and maintained at the site of fatal car accidents to commemorate the dead. Another example are the vigils and meals that families organize at the gravesites of deceased loved ones on the Day of the Dead, 'conversing, remembering, reconciling, and updating them on what has happened to their family and friends since the last visit.'[25]

Leader offers a different but complementary interpretation of my ritual when he writes that most burial and mourning rituals include a stage in which the mourners give up a part of themselves, for instance by throwing a lock of hair or a precious object into the grave. He asks whether these symbolic sacrifices are made in order to remain bound to the dead, or, on the contrary, to achieve separation. Answering his own question, he asserts that these small symbolic sacrifices indicate a positive act. 'As if in addition to what we are forced to lose, we add another loss, as if to positivize it, as if we are *consenting* to the loss rather than refusing it.'[26]

As I have said before in this book—and have illustrated with many examples—artists are particularly good at creating rituals for themselves and others, generating material or physical expressions of unacknowledged loss. This is true even for the most difficult and devastating losses, such as losing a child. The Flemish scenographer Valentine Kempynck, whose work I discussed in a previous chapter, built one of her 'small benches' for a couple who separated after going through an abortion. The bench marked the 'space' and 'time' they once shared. Since there was no child that represented their union, they also had little birthmarks tattooed on their bodies 'so that they could touch and caress it.'[27]

Grief for the loss of a child does not always lead to breakups or the dissolution of existing family constellations. It can also deepen a relationship. The philosopher Will Daddario and his wife, the literary scholar Joanne Zerdy, experienced the stillbirth of their first son, Finlay Emilio. Afterwards, Daddario wrote an essay for the online journal *Performance Philosophy*. He describes *To Grieve* as 'a set of instructions for my future self in order to grieve openly.'[28] This is the opposite of what Knapp calls 'shadow grief.'

For Daddario, Finlay's death was the last in a long line of deaths that came in short succession, including Will's father, grandmother, a close friend, and his animal companion. He defines his grief as 'the gravity of the social,'[29] which obliged him to rebuild his world. 'I must allow the weight of grief to shape my vision of the world and of myself in the world.'[30] This rebuilding happens on all levels and imposes a series of existential questions, including: 'What time will grief make, and what will you make within grief's duration?'[31] Related to this is the question, 'how will you create a new vernacular to talk about this loss?' He also addresses the fundamental difference in experience between him and Joanna.

> I also knew that I needed help to understand that which I couldn't possibly understand, the experience my wife felt as the doctor told her that Finlay's heart had stopped beating ... the need to continue living without the life she had been growing inside of her for forty weeks.[32]

Together, they created the organization *Inviting Abundance*[33] 'to promote the cultivation of a creative grief practice of embracing and transforming the pain.' One of the organization's initiatives is the creation of a podcast in which various people, many of them artists, talk about the importance of grieving openly, actively, and purposely. In the first podcast episode, Daddario and Zerdy describe in detail how they each experienced the pregnancy, the labor, and the realization that their first-born son had died. 'I say to Joanne that we are grieving together alone. She says we are grieving alone together. When we acknowledge both to be true, we re-member each other to ourselves and become a plural-singularity within grief.'[34] Seeing a roadside shrine, Joanna reflects how her body became a similar marker of the boundary between life and death. Embracing their grief also meant creating a new beginning for themselves. They moved to another place, where eventually their other sons, Phalen and Ren were born. The podcast series encompasses a diverse range of topics such as rock 'n' roll and grief, herbs and grief, death and grief doulas,[35] and grief and social justice.

My good friend, the Toronto-based choreographer Andrea Nann, was seven months pregnant with her son Owen when her daughter Chi Lin, who was almost three at the time, died. Andrea dedicated several of her choreographic works to the memory of her daughter, also as a way of coming to terms with her own mourning process. Andrea worked with her close friend and long-time collaborator, the Canadian choreographer Sarah Chase. Together they created *A Crazy Kind of Hope* (2013), a solo work conceived and directed by Sarah, performed by Andrea, and presented in Sarah's unique dance-storytelling form. As part of the creation process Sarah devised polyrhythmic movement puzzles and cyclical movement patterns to provoke private memories and personal stories from Andrea.

The first story in *A Crazy Kind of Hope* is that of Andrea's uncle Wayne, a potter, who buys a carp at the market for his dinner, only to discover after a seven-hour-long journey back home that the carp is still alive. Instead of preparing and eating the fish, he digs a hole in his garden and the carp becomes the first inhabitant in a very populated fishpond, which also has hundreds of waterlilies floating in it. Andrea tells the story while standing on a small bench, which turns out to have a lid. She opens the lid, takes out two lotus flowers and performs a dance lying down with a flower in each hand, moving in spirals across the floor.

At the end of this dance, she returns the flowers to their resting place and sits down on the bench. The stage lights accentuate the floating effect of the movements of her legs. On the soundtrack, we hear the waves of the ocean. She tells us about her son Owen, who is 19 now,[36] and explains the meaning behind the name of her daughter: *Chi* means 'life-force' in Mandarin and *Lin* is Cantonese for 'lotus flower.' Andrea recalls a journey she and her husband Andy undertook when Chi Lin was only six weeks old, driving her to see the ocean for the first time. The sound of the waves calmed her and 'she looked like a buddha, watching over us.' She also smiled for the first time, which filled her parents with 'a crazy kind of hope, but we really didn't know for what.'[37] After Chi Lin's death, Andrea contacts her uncle Wayne and asks him to make an urn for her ashes. He creates an urn in the shape of a lotus bud. The exhibition *Mourning: On Loss and Change* (2020) at the Hamburger Kunsthalle also featured a series of urns created by two Ghanaian artists, Ataa Oko and Kudjoe Affutu. Each urn had its own particular shape: a tiger, a shoe, a rice sack, a car. It is part of a popular trend in Ghana to use coffins that are shaped and painted with images that refer to the deceased's personality, profession, or personal passions.

In the solo, Andrea weaves the different threads of her story into a complex, non-linear web of dances. After the lotus flower dance and the re-membering of her daughter's name, there is a dance made up of two phrases, one for each arm. One is dedicated to her daughter and one to her son. The two children 'never actually met,' but they are now dancing together. *A Crazy Kind of Hope* ends with a dance in which Andrea combines a phrase made up of eleven movements with another phrase made up of nine. Eleven times nine equals 99. Chi Lin, who died in 1999, lived exactly 999 days. 'In the end our daughter was with us much longer than anyone could have predicted.'[38]

In Schneider's *A Beginner's Guide to Constructing the Universe*, he explains that 'the ancient mathematical philosophers called nine the "finishing post" and "that which brings completion."'[39] In many languages 'nine' and 'new' are associated. In numerical terms, ten follows the sense of completion of nine, symbolizing new beginnings. 'It is a new beginning, a journey into limitlessness.'[40] By dancing, Andrea consciously activates this numerical symbolism to extend the presence of her daughter beyond her death.

So if I were to start a looping phrase of eleven gestures with my left hand and then add to it a looping phrase of nine gestures with my right hand, then after 99 possible combinations I would find myself at the end of the cycle or back at the beginning, starting all over again.[41]

# Notes

1 The title of this chapter references Judith Savage's book *Mourning Unlived Lives* (1989, 2018).
2 One of the traditional *moirolói* that Katerina Zakka sang in *Dakrisména Póulia*.
3 Lewis 1961, 2015, p. 93.
4 Kessler 2019, p. 150.
5 Samuel 2017, p. 174.
6 Leader 2009, p. 85.
7 Savage 1989, 2018, p. 101.
8 Ibid., p. xii.
9 Ibid., pp. 6–7.
10 Assmann 2000, p. 44.
11 Ibid., p. 50.
12 Savage 1989, 2018, p. 62.
13 Kessler 2019, p. 153.
14 I wrote about some of these personal experiences of migrating in *In-Between Dance Cultures* (2015).
15 Kang 2017, p. 17.
16 Ibid., p. 37.
17 Ibid., p. 131.
18 Ibid., p. 145.
19 From the performance text of *The Narrator*.
20 Ibid.
21 Ibid.
22 Ibid.
23 Bays 2003, p. 38.
24 McGuire 2008, p. 57.
25 Ibid., p. 58.
26 Leader 2009, p. 135.
27 From an unpublished lecture by Kempynck.
28 From the introductory episode of the podcast series *To Grieve, Inviting Abundance—To Grieve Podcast* focused on creative dimensions of grief.
29 Daddario 2015, p. 266.
30 Ibid., 267.
31 Ibid., 270.
32 Ibid., 277.
33 See: www.invitingabudance.net.
34 Daddario 2015, 278.
35 A doula is a trained companion who is not a healthcare professional and who supports another individual through a significant health-related experience, such as childbirth, miscarriage, induced abortion or stillbirth, or non-reproductive experiences such as dying (source: Wikipedia).
36 *A Crazy kind of Hope* was restaged in 2019 as part of a larger program entitled *All of Our Dreaming*, in which several of Andrea's artistic partners, including her husband, the musician Andy Maize, share their own stories of loss.
37 From the performance text of *A Crazy Kind of Hope*.
38 Ibid.
39 Schneider 1994, p. 302.
40 Ibid., 324.
41 From the performance text of *A Crazy Kind of Hope*.

# Lamenting the Future

> Let the pain become a sound,
> A living river on the breath.
> Raise your voice.
> Cry out. Scream. Wail.
> Keen and mourn
> For the dismembering of the world.[1]

When I started giving workshops to guide people in writing their own laments, I was both surprised and touched that some of the participants in their mid-twenties weren't so much concerned about lamenting past losses, but felt they had to lament the lack of opportunities and possibilities in their future. It was a big eye-opener.

When the global Covid-19 lockdown hit us in the spring of 2020, my first engagement to be moved online was a course I had been scheduled to teach at the theater department of the University of Ottawa on how to 'perform mourning.' The group I should be working with was made up of four talented students from the MFA program in theater directing. My original plan had been to have them write their own lament in the form of a script for a short monologue. We would have then explored all its performative potentials (such as the underlying musicality of the language or the physicality that it might elicit) and investigated how the form could both support and contain an emotional release. When the course moved online, it felt more appropriate to use a medium that we were obliged to use anyway, so I proposed for them to create short videos instead.

One of the students, Guillaume Saindon, had already completed an MA in film directing and felt more at home with the new format. When I asked the students for references and sources of inspiration, Guillaume chose Mark Fisher's book *Ghosts of My Life: Writing on Depression, Hauntology and Lost Futures* (2014). In it, Fisher applies Derrida's notion of hauntology to his critique of twenty-first-century culture, particularly music culture. Fisher defines haunting as 'a failed mourning. It is about refusing to give up the ghost or—and this can sometimes amount to the same thing—the refusal of the ghost to give up on us.'[2] He references Franco 'Bifo' Berardi's book *After the Future* (2011) and his notion of 'the slow cancellation of the future.' Berardi argues that the myth of progressive modernity has become obsolete and that the cult of the new has been replaced with a nostalgic recycling of the past.

Fisher offers plenty of examples of where this can be heard in twenty-first-century music production:

> While 20th-century experimental culture was seized by a recombinatorial delirium, which made it feel as if newness was infinitely available, the 21st century is oppressed by a crushing sense of finitude and exhaustion. It doesn't feel like the future. Or, alternatively, it doesn't feel as if the 21st century has started yet. We remain trapped in the 20th century.[3]

Confronted with the Covid-19 lockdown, Guillaume reflected on how 'the act of creating, while in a global crisis, is very contradictory. How not knowing what or how. How not being able to do anything, not being able to move, he still had to produce.'[4] Inspired by music by the post-soviet Estonian rapper Tommy Cash and the French techno-punks Casual Gabberz, which he would listen to late at night, Guillaume wrote a lament for his 'lost future.'

> Iiiiiiii ii ii i. Mmmm. No.
> I no longer. No. Hmmm.
> I no longer have hopes for love parades
> For demonstrations
> For functioning marriages
> For renewable energies
> For disarmament
> For work opportunities ...
> For my parents
> To have children
> For my teacher in sixth grade who said I would have a bright future
> For the one of grade twelve, who said exactly the same ...
> I am tired
> I am not naïve anymore
> I am disillusioned
> I am violent
> I am tired of waiting
> I am not with you, nor with them
> I am frightened
> I don't have a future
> I have no more hope
> I need you to tell me that everything will be fine, one day[5]

The short video that illustrates the lament is a frantic loop in black-and-white that repeatedly scans Guillaume's desk. 'My desk. Monolith of online work. A keyboard. Two screens. A mouse. Post-its. Invoices. And sometimes dirty dishes. My desk. An extension of my present condition ... One day it will stick to my body like a Cronenberg mutation.'[6] Guillaume's body is only present in the video as a ghostly portrait on the screens or as a shadow of a hand manipulating the mouse. He recites his lament, mixing his voice with a computer-generated female voice, which adds to the eerie quality of the film. At one point, the loop seems to become stuck. There is a brief moment of release, both visually and acoustically, when the camera captures a view of the street through the window. Piano music and audible breathing can be heard as we get a glimpse of the spring landscape outside. But the black shadow of the hand quickly obscures the view and the loop continues. The video ends with a view of Guillaume's ghost on the screen, covering his face with his hands in desperation.

In June 2020, HAU Hebbel am Ufer Berlin planned a second edition of the project *Unacknowledged Loss*, which had been curated by Barbara Raes (see also chapter 'Laments to Dialogue with Those Who Are Absent'). Nine Berlin-based artists were invited to develop new rituals for dealing with loss. Because of the Covid-19 lockdown, the artists weren't able to meet in person. Instead, they worked individually on their rituals, which were then filmed by the artist Liz Rosenfeld.[7] At least two of the nine artists developed a ritual that explicitly addressed the loss of a future. In *Extinct*, Enis Turan sits on an empty stage in a meditative pose while 130 candles burn down and 75 ice cubes slowly melt. He builds a small tree out of 280 wooden sticks which he plants in a pile of soil at the end of the ritual. It is a farewell to all the raw materials that the earth has lost in just one year:

> 750 billion tons of ice have melted due to global warming; 28 million hectares of forest have been cut down or burned; 400 million hectares of land have been degraded, of which 120 million hectares have turned into desert; ... I am deeply sorry for this massive loss.[8]

In *A Farewell to Melancholy Futures*, Olympia Bukkakis also meditates on an empty stage, in drag, while reciting all her lost futures:

<blockquote>

I lose multiple futures every day, every day since I was born
When I was 13 months old, I lost the future in which I knew
my biological father ...
When I was 24, I lost the future in which I continue to live
in my home country ...
In March of this year, I lost the future in which I could touch
people without fear of infection ...
I lose many futures every day[9]

</blockquote>

The emotion of anger comes up regularly in any mourning process. Often it is anger at the injustice of events, as in the examples I described in the previous chapter, where the natural order of things seems to be reversed. Why did (s)he have to die? Why is this happening to me? If the death is a violent one, such as in an accident or even worse, the result of a killing, this anger is often also the fuel for a cry or demand for justice or even revenge.

In Mani, the region of the Southern Peloponnese where the *moirológhia* are still practiced today, a culture of vendetta also survived well into the twentieth century. It involved families killing members of other families in revenge for previous killings. The laments played an important part in this, as they were often used by the women to urge their male relatives to take responsibility for defending the family's honor.

Seen in this light, it is no coincidence that the present-day discourse on mourning within the Black Lives Matter movement and similar movements against structural police and state violence, such as for instance in Palestine, often highlights the anger that is part of grief as an important source of energy and motivation for further action. The final section of Rebeca Solnit's collection of essays on the current crises in the world, *Call Them by Their True Names* (2018), is called 'Possibilities.' In it, she offers valuable insights into the positive aspects and results of activism. In a speech to future journalists, she stresses the importance of breaking the story, of making visible what was locked out of view. Another essay in this final section is called 'Hope in Grief.' There she acknowledges that the sorrow and anger of grief are powerful catalysts for change. She reiterates the same belief in the final essay 'In Praise of Indirect Consequences,' quoting Patrisse Cullors, one of the founders of Black Lives Matter, who describes the movement's mission as 'rooted in grief and rage but pointed towards visions and dreams.'[10]

In her book *Rebellious Mourning: The Collective Work of Grief* (2017), the American writer and activist Cindy Milstein brings together a diverse, inspired, and moving collection of testimonials on how processes of mourning can lead to engaged resistance against structural violence such as racism or homophobia. It contains 'firsthand, frontline stories' about Black Lives Matter activists and other victims of violence in the United States, Canada, and Mexico, including testimonies from some of the parents of the 43 Mexican students of Ayotzninapa who disappeared after they were kidnapped by the Mexican police in 2015. Also heard are voices of Syrian refugees, Palestinian martyrs, and relatives of victims of the Fukushima nuclear disaster, and of people who died of AIDS because of poor conditions and negligence in the US prison system. In her introduction to the collection Milstein references a question that Judith Butler asks in *Precarious Life* (2004): why is it that certain lives seem to have more worth than others, both to be lived and to be grieved? Butler wrote her collection of essays in the immediate aftermath of September 11, 2001, and 'in response to the conditions of heightened vulnerability and aggression that followed from those events.'[11]

> Some lives are grievable, and others are not; the differential allocation of grievability that decides what kind of subject is and must be grieved, and which kind of subject must not, operates to produce and maintain certain exclusionary conceptions of who is normatively human: what counts as a liveable life and a grievable death?[12]

In Butler's more recent thinking and writing, for example in *The Force of Nonviolence* (2020), the notion of grievability continues to be at the center of her ethics of radical equality. 'One normative aspiration of this work is to contribute to the formulation of a political imaginary of the radical equality of grievability.'[13] Butler argues that in our present-day reality, lives are valued differently and that this difference in valuation is most noticeable in 'the radically unequal distribution of grievability,'[14] that is, the way that 'lives are deemed to be more or less grievable.'[15]

> To be grievable is to be interpellated in such a way that you know your life matters; that the loss of your life would matter; that your body is treated as one that

<blockquote>should be able to live and thrive, whose precarity should be minimized, for which provisions for flourishing should be available. The presumption of equal grievability would be … a principle that organizes the social organization of health, food, shelter, employment, sexual life and civic life.[16]</blockquote>

Butler also expands the notion of grievability to other non-human live forms. 'This means that we have to think not only about persons, but animals; and not only about living creatures, but living processes, the systems and forms of life.'[17] She argues that all life forms have the right to be mourned and to engage in processes of mourning themselves. 'What of lakes. glaciers, or trees? Surely they can be mourned, and they can, as material realities, conduct the work of mourning as well.'[18] Butler references Greek tragedy in her work, drawing attention to the ways it uses the lament form as a form of activism capable of turning mourning into protest. 'In Greek tragedy, lament seems to follow rage and is usually belated. But sometimes there is a chorus … who lament in advance, mourning as soon as they see it coming.'[19] The above examples of laments by the younger generation resemble such a chorus.

Most of the authors in Milstein's book practice a militant form of mourning. They frequently reiterate Butler's question, asking why some lives are seen as grievable and others are not. 'What makes certain deaths worthy of grieving? How do some names turn into calls for action, and why are others swiftly forgotten?'[20] While Butler sees a possible 'appeal to a "we"' for all of us have some notion of what it is to have lost somebody,'[21] Milstein stresses the uniqueness of each loss and each mourning process. Her book

<blockquote>tries not to homogenize or universalize the myriad of losses, individual and social. Their gamut and magnitude—from colonialism to incarceration, climate catastrophe to poverty, rape to chronic illness, one's culture to one's dignity—play out on different bodies in different brutal ways.[22]</blockquote>

And even if her collection of diverse stories 'sits with the heaviness we feel in a world that, we're told, has not future,'[23] it also offers counter-narratives of how collectively remembering someone's death is a powerful strategy for resistance.

The graphic designer Jeff Clark collected a series of portraits for Milstein's book, which were created by graphic designers and graffiti artists to commemorate people who were killed on the streets. He points out that in French *faire grève* (to strike) is etymologically linked to 'grief' by means of 'grievance' and the Latin *gravare* (to be burdened):

The public artists in the pages that follow have made of grieving a grievance—a visual strike—proving it's possible to transmute some of the weight of mourning those murdered by the state into an act that is simultaneously memorial and protest.[24]

*Bilderschlachten* (2019) by the German choreographer Stephanie Thiersch, created in close collaboration with composer Brigitta Muntendorf, starts with a 15-minute prologue in which the orchestra plays while scattered among the audience in the auditorium, creating a surround sound effect. Meanwhile the dancers, all in black, move together very slowly, as if they were interconnected micro-organisms. They are joined on stage by the members of the Asasello String Quartet. A lighting change transforms the environment from dark to blue with a warm yellow spotlight, creating the effect of a sunrise over a projected globe. The general atmosphere is one of suspension—a liminal, in-between state.

After this overture, there is a blackout. When the lights come up again, they reveal the dancers in colorful outfits made out of plastic and latex, parts of which slowly blow up into amorphous shapes. The humorous ballet that follows celebrates the diversity of the species. The dancers start peeling off layer after layer of their costumes, returning to more anthropomorphic forms. Nonsensical sounds seem to prefigure the emergence of language. Eventually everyone comes together in a shared work-out routine. In the next part of the piece, this colorful universe transforms again into a monochromatic landscape of blacks and grays. The performers have taken up their full human identities, with the exception of the string quartet, who still wear left-overs of the colorful plastic costumes, draped across their bodies as waste. The dancers connect through heavy breathing, which turns into rhythmic chanting of slogans and escalates into a tribal war dance performed by a mob. They then start dropping to the floor and crawling around, accompanied by recordings of bird song mixed with the musical fragments played live by the orchestra and the string quartet. A microphone is passed around, mixing the dancers' voices into the artfully composed cacophony, which becomes a unison chant: 'You have to die for your government, for your country. That is shit!'

At its very climax, the music transitions into a deconstruction of Chopin's funeral march, during which the performers are joined on stage by all the members of the orchestra, forming an impressive mass of 53 people. The amplified voices of individual performers comment on the apocalyptic ending: 'The people of the future!,' 'This is the end!' Walking in simple patterns, they repeat a series of ritual hand gestures. The ritual of mourning is the culmination of a performance that started out by celebrating the exuberant and colorful diversity of the species, went on to witness its extinction in a monochromatic black landscape, and ended by finally mourning its losses. The march ends with everyone lying down on stage in a huge pile of corpses, from which only the sounds of the Asasello String Quartet reverberate.

> As the wailing and steadily instrumentation of Chopin's funeral march plays, the dancers begin to bewail. In the end, when all that is playing is a harp and four double basses, trying to maintain the melody to their highest flageolets, it becomes impossible to conceal the agony and suffering in the production of sound. It is the final farewell that connects people; it is the realization that meanings disappear or unremittingly transform.[25]

Donna J. Haraway's speculative feminism in *Staying with the Trouble: Making Kin in the Chtulucene* (2016) has been an important inspiration for *Bilderschlachten*. In it, Haraway argues for a radical ecological and feminist critique and an approach in which we have to take up our shared 'response-ability' for the whole planet and for all its species—or critters, as Haraway calls them in her poetic language—including those that have already become extinct. Haraway references the ecological philosopher Thom van Dooren who, in his book *Flight Ways: Life and Loss at the Edge of Extinction* (2014), discusses 'bird species living on the extended edge of extinction.'[26] 'Van Dooren proposes that mourning is intrinsic to cultivating response-ability.'[27] He argues that it is the notion of human exceptionalism—i.e., the fact that we consider ourselves unique as a species, different from the rest of the animal kingdom, because of for instance our language skills, our moral agency, or our 'knowledge of death'—'that holds us distant, intellectually and emotionally, from our more than human world.'[28] Van Dooren gives many examples of animals displaying grief such as foxes burying others or gorillas, elephants, and crows mourning and taking care of their dead: 'Perhaps the ability to live in a way that references and interacts with the dead is not uniquely human *as such*, but rather is a way of life that we are increasingly denying to a host of other animals.'[29] He concludes:

> Perhaps in the end, what must me mourned at this time, alongside so many other things, is the diminishment of mourning itself, the loss of the rich and varied expressions of grief that have evolved on this planet over millions of years.[30]

> Mourning is about dwelling with a loss and so coming to appreciate what it means, how the world has changed, and how we must ourselves change and renew our relationships if we are to move forward from here. In this context, genuine mourning should open us into an awareness of our dependence on and relationships with those countless others being driven over the edge of extinction.[31]

But what if a generation growing up with a fear of climate change and other global cataclysms already feels the need to mourn future absences that it hasn't actually experienced yet? In a column in *The New York Times*,[32] the American reporter Cara Buckley describes how she took part in a workshop called 'Cultivating active hope: living with joy amidst the climate crisis' in an attempt to deal with her 'climate angst.' From this workshop experience she formulates a prescription for 'handling climate grief': her call to 'embrace the pain' paraphrases Haraway's phrase, 'stay with the trouble.' One of the workshop facilitators summed up Buckley's grief with a quote by the pioneering environmental grief activist Joanna Macy: 'Our pain for what is happening is the other side of the coin of our love for the world ... We feel such depths of despair because we love the planet so much.'[33]

 *Bilderschlachten* reflects this dichotomy of love and pain. First it celebrates our love for all the critters of this planet, then it embraces the pain of their loss, and eventually it exteriorizes our grief into a ritual of mourning—a funeral march. For me, the final scene of *Bilderschlachten* triggered another memory of funeral marches. Many years ago, I was in Trapani, a city on the western coast of Sicily, in the week leading up to Easter. One early evening, several local brass bands gathered in the squares in front of the various parish churches to rehearse a repertoire of funeral marches for the annual Procession of the Mysteries, which takes place every Good Friday. While the brass bands rehearsed, members of each congregation gathered in and outside of the church to burn candles and decorate the statues with flowers, but mainly to be together, celebrate, and mourn.

The brass bands and the collective rituals of mourning created an atmosphere that illustrated to me the importance of being together and sharing the 'response-ability' for our losses, in order to be able to heal ourselves and regenerate, both on an individual level and collectively. In this case, the rituals were based on Christian traditions, but they also carried within them the remnants of much older pagan rituals celebrating death and resurrection as part of the natural cycle of seasons. Milstein ends her collection of stories on militant grief with a plea for remembering to celebrate such natural cycles and losses:

> Only because we fight—against losses that shouldn't happen, and for spaces to grieve together in cities that increasingly isolate us and care for nothing. We fight not only for quality of life. We struggle for quality of death, for lives and death of our own making and mourning. We battle for a return to natural loss, such as change of seasons and the seasons of life.[34]

All the artists mentioned in this book perform their mourning, that is, they create forms that express their emotions of grief. And because these forms are stylized, characterized by a certain artifice, they are able to contain and (to an extent) control the grief. The lament form is particularly suitable for this because it combines both language and non-language (i.e., stylized sighs, sobs, and an embodied physical language that supports the affective qualities of the voice). The laments are not only used to express one's own emotions, but also to give a voice to the departed, enabling them to answer back. By doing so, they offer them another kind of presence, even agency, to continue to dialogue and act with the

living. The lament also invites the community to witness the mourning and turn the individual narrative of grief into a 'dialogue of mournings.' This dialogue has the potential to become militant. The re-membering of the absence can become a call to action, and a catalyst for change.

# Notes

1   Lines from a song by the twenty-first-century neopagan witch Starhawk, quoted in Haraway 2016, p. 166.
2   Fisher 2014, p. 22.
3   Ibid., p. 8.
4   From the unpublished essay by Guillaume Saindon, 'Prose on Being a means of production while you and everyone you know is confined' (2020).
5   Guillaume Saindon's original text:
    Jeeeeeee ee ee e. Mmmm. Non.
    Je n'est plus. Non. Hmmm.
    Je n'est plus les espoirs des
    loves-parades
    des manifestations
    des mariages fonctionnels
    des énergies renouvelables
    du désarmements
    des opportunité d'emplois ...
    de mes parents
    d'avoir des enfants
    de ma prof de maternelle qui m'a
    dit que j'avais un bel avenir
    puis de celle de douzième qui a
    dit la même chose ...
    Je est épuisé
    Je est plus naïf
    Je est désillusioné
    Je est violent
    Je est tanné d'attendre
    Je est sans toi, ni eux, ni elles
    Je est angoissé
    Je est sans avenir
    Je n'est plus espoir.
    J'ai besoin de toi qui me dit que
    tout ira bien un jour peut-être.
6   From the unpublished essay by Guillaume Saindon, 'Prose on Being a means of production while you and everyone you know is confined' (2020).
7   All nine short films are available to watch on HAU Hebbel am Ufer's YouTube channel: youtube.com/user/321HAU/videos.
8   From the voice over of Enis Turan video, youtube.com/user/321HAU/videos
9   From the video by Olympia Bukkakis and Liz Rosenfeld, youtube.com/watch?v=BAJHocx7SvY.
10   Solnit 2018, p. 175.
11   Butler 2004, p. XI.
12   Ibid., p. XIV–XV.
13   Butler 2020, p. 74.
14   Ibid., p. 75.
15   Ibid., p. 73.
16   Ibid., p. 59.
17   Ibid., p. 58.
18   Ibid., p.76.
19   Ibid., p. 102.
20   Hussan in Milstein 2017, p. 64.
21   Butler 2004, p. 20.
22   Milstein 2017, p. 7.
23   Ibid., p. 7.
24   Clark in Milstein 2017, p. 205.
25   Muntendorf in Thiersch 2020, p. 49.
26   Haraway 2016, p. 38.
27   Ibid , p. 38.
28   Van Dooren 2014, p. 126.
29   Ibid , p. 133.
30   Ibid , p. 137.
31   Haraway 2016, pp. 38–39.
32   Buckley 2019.
33   Serrante in Buckley 2019.
34   Milstein 2017, p. 402.

# Coda:
# On Lullabies

Ocean Vuong's poetic autobiographical novel *On Earth We're Briefly Gorgeous* (2019) is a letter to his mother in which he describes their shared experiences, hers of growing up in post-war Vietnam and his of growing up in the United States after they emigrated. It ends with a journey back to their roots in order to bury the ashes of his grandmother. While staying in a hotel in Saigon he witnesses an improvised wake where the laments are a series of karaoke songs performed by drag queens.



He goes on to recall 'how music was the sound of a woman wailing' and how he already heard this when he was still inside the womb. 'It was a Vietnamese lullaby. How every lullaby began with wailing, as if pain could not exit the body any other way.'[3]

For several years now, I have used a particular voice practice to warm up my vocal cords without putting too much stress on them. I learnt this practice from my colleague Lin Snelling, who learnt it from Ann Dyer, whose teachings are rooted in Nada yoga, the yoga of sound. The practice involves vocalizing different vowels on the out breath while shifting your awareness to different parts of the body that correspond to the chakra system. Having done the practice for many years, both on my own and with diverse groups of participants in my workshops, I have an experiential understanding of the effects of its vibrational qualities: how the different sounds affect individual parts of the body and how somatic resonances and connections are created among the people who are practicing together. Jan Chozen Bays writes that similar resonances appear when mantras are being chanted aloud in the Buddhist tradition. Another function of such mantras is to support us in times of emotional distress. 'In our fear and grief the mind becomes a wailing, chaotic thing at a time when we most need to rest and have clarity. This is when a mantra can help.'[4]

As well as using stylized cries and sobs, traditional laments such as the *moirológhia* often 'cut' or abbreviate words in unusual places in order to lengthen the vowels. The emotional resonance of the voice is most audible in the vowels. Even in the preverbal stages of our development, as infants and before we have required any other language skills, we use 'ah' and 'oh' to express pain, pleasure, or surprise. These vowels carry emotion and allow it to be expressed and shared on a somatic and energetic level. The same vowels can be used to soothe and calm small children. Nowhere is this more evident than in lullabies.

In her music therapy analysis, Xanthoula Dakovanou references the French psychoanalyst Didier Anzieu, saying that 'the melodic bath (the voice of the mother, her songs, the music she listens to) provides the infant with a first sound mirror,'[5] which, in analogy with Lacan's mirror image, helps it to form and become conscious of a Self.

> The first melody emitted by this voice becomes a vocal and transitional space game for the baby, functioning as a bond with the mother and as a consolation for separation. This state of lack and grieving in later life opens up possibilities for sublimation of the libido in artistic forms of creation—and what would be a better link to the lost object than the voice, the first sonorous link to it![6]

My oldest son, Filip, was born in 1985 when I was still at university, finishing my original degree in theater studies. While completing my theoretical studies, I would occasionally also take workshops organized by the Centre of Experimental Theatre at the university. It offered practical research laboratories, most of which were connected to the emerging field of theater anthropology and were taught by collaborators of Grotowski or Barba. Among the workshops I participated in was a voice workshop given by Toni Cots, who was still an active member of Barba's Odin Teatret at the time. We were given the task of learning a song in a language we didn't know, in order to play with the sounds without being distracted by their meaning. I learnt an African song of which I had a recording, about *Ninke Nanke*, a mythological creature that is half-snake, half-dragon, popular in West-African countries such as The Gambia, Guinea, and Senegal. The song was particularly useful for the practice because it consisted of a chorus of only vowels, which can be loosely transcribed as 'aa i a o wa jo i a o o wa nex.' The verses tell the story of *Ninke Nanke*. In that workshop I realized for the first time that sounds, and particularly vowels, have their own vibrational and energetic qualities. Since it was one of the few songs I knew by heart, I also started to use it as a lullaby for my two sons, Filip and Steven. Thirty years later, I still sing it to my youngest son Julian.

In his book *Good Vibrations: Die heilende Kraft der Musik* (The healing power of music, 2019), the psychologist and neuroscientist Stefan Kölsch gives an overview of recent scientific research on the therapeutic potentials of music. He discusses, among other things, the use of lullabies in supporting premature babies. The calming effects of lullabies can help to regulate their heartbeat and their respiration. Kölsch also notes the universal acoustic and musical characteristics of lullabies: 'Everywhere in the world, these songs sound similar: the melodies often go down, they are constructed relatively simply and are repetitive.'[7] In music therapy studies, the term 'lullament' is used to describe how the soothing quality of the lullaby not only supports infants in crossing over from wakefulness to sleep, but can also be applied in palliative care to support the transition from life to death.[8]

One of the reasons why I traveled to Hamburg to see the exhibition *Mourning: On Loss and Change* at the Kunsthalle was to see the work of the Scottish artist Susan Philipsz. Philipsz creates sound installations from 'found' sounds. She re-enacts songs or fragments of compositions that have some historical relevance to the architecture and the urban settings she places them in. Often these sounds are connected to the theme of death. The ways in which they are projected into empty spaces also evoke eerie resonances with the ghosts of the past. The Hamburg exhibition included Philipsz' famous piece *Lowlands*, for which she received the Turner Prize in 2010. *Lowlands* was originally shown in Berlin (2008) and Glasglow (2010). Philipsz recorded three different versions of a well-known Scottish seamen's shanty that started out as a lament sung for a drowned lover. In Glasgow, the different versions were broadcast under three bridges. Philipsz' choice of the location had been inspired by her discovery of a memorial for a suicide under one of the bridges. In Berlin, the sound installation dialogued with a video installation commemorating Rosa Luxemburg at the site where her body was found, the Landwehrkanal. Although the corner room in the Hamburger Kunsthalle where the piece was installed for the exhibition was well chosen, all of its windows looking out over the waters of the nearby Alster, the installation didn't have the same impact in the museum context as it did in its original locations. Philipsz had also been commissioned to create a new work for the entrance hall of the Kunsthalle. For this commission she chose the Irish song *Keen for a Dead Child*, in a version by the folk singer Kitty Gallagher, which she deconstructed and stripped down to a very short sound fragment. It was only broadcast once every hour in the empty atrium space.

> The keen reminded me of a mantra, with the same tones being repeated over and over. I have stripped the music down to its barest elements and concentrated on the sounds of the individual tones. I have recorded them in my own voice and arranged them in ascending and descending scales. The sound emerges from four different levels of the atrium, rising and falling in rhythmic patterns.[9]

The waiting and anticipation, followed by the very uneventful sound, provoked a feeling of emptiness that resembled the 'black holes' of grief. For a previous commission for the Pro Arte Foundation in Finland, Philipsz had created a similar effect of a minimal sound in a large empty space, the South Hall of Helsinki's Central Station. Entitled *When Day Closes* (2010), her installation used fragments of the lullaby *Sydämeni laulu* (Song of My Heart), which has almost acquired national anthem status in Finland in its choral arrangement by Jean Sibelius. This lullaby belongs to a category of Finnish lullabies known as *Tuonela* lullabies. *Tuonela* in Finnish mythology is the kingdom of the dead, which is reached by crossing the river Tuoni. *Song of My Heart* is 'a positive death wish lullaby.'[10] The lullaby becomes a lament in which the mother wishes that her child might die, in order to wake up in the afterlife, which is considered a place of solace compared with the hardships of this world. Philipsz was aware 'that these lullabies may have developed as modes of elaborating the fears caused by the high rate of children's deaths in the cold and harsh living conditions of Northern Europe before the twentieth century.'[11]

The public sound installation *When Day Closes* was preceded by another project, *After Closedown* (2009), in which a

Finnish television channel broadcast two recordings of Philipsz singing lullabies from cult horror movies at the end of their regular programming: Robin Hardy's *The Wicker Man* (1973) and the lullaby theme from Roman Polański's *Rosemary's Baby* (1968). 'Philipsz evokes and enacts around a semiotic field of associations involving childhood, singing, the political dimension of pain, poverty, child death in Northern Europe, she takes the position of the weeping, singing mother.'[12] Reading about Philipsz' bridging of lullaby and lament reminded me of the Yiddish lament that Sidi Larbi Cherkaoui sings at the end of *zero degrees*, which actually goes back to a Basque lullaby.

During one of my return visits to Montreal in 2018, I recorded the *Ninke Nanke* 'lullaby' for the project *Les Berceurs du Temps*, which had been initiated by my colleague and friend, the Canadian-Russian dramaturg Ilya Krouglikov. Ilya created *Les Berceurs du Temps* together with his artistic collaborators Sara Dell'Ava and Wolfram Sander in 2016. Their starting point for the work was a local custom that had prevailed until their parent's generation. At the time, most homes in Québec had beautiful hand-made rocking chairs carved out of wood, which can now be found very cheaply in second-hand stores. They bought several dozens of these chairs in different sizes and installed a set of mini speakers in each chair, which would offer a private listening experience to the people sitting and rocking in them. The installation was then presented in public spaces such as libraries or parks, with the chairs as its 'hardware.' The 'software,' i.e., the songs that were played in each chair, were all recordings of lullabies from many different cultures and in many different languages. Their diversity was designed to mirror the multi-ethnic population of Montreal. 'We invite the passerby to contemplate the past through the lullabies of the world ... to better imagine a future in which all the voices, even those who disappeared, continue to resonate.'[13] Whenever the installation is presented, an old VW minibus with a recording studio built into travels with it. Anyone who visits the installation is invited to record their own lullaby. The installation and living archive, *Lulling Time*, has already collected more than a thousand lullabies in 55 different languages.[14]

Robert Pogue Harrison, whose book *The Dominion of the Dead* has been a huge inspiration on my journey, starts his introduction by stating that 'the dead and the unborn are native allies.' The former haunt 'the living with guilt, dread, and a sense of responsibility, obliging us, by whatever means necessary, to take the unborn into care and to keep the story going, even if we never quite figure out what the story is about.'[15] The personal journey I have described in this book started more than fifty years ago with the unexpected death of my father. It became a more conscious research process twenty years ago, when I discovered the *moirológhia* in Epirus, Greece. The journey, in which I am mainly a temporary custodian, merely a link between the dead and the unborn, continues.

# Notes

1   King 2018, p. 219.
2   Vuong 2019, p. 226.
3   Ibid., p. 227.
4   Bays 2002, p. 210.
5   Dakovanou 2012, 2013, pp. 29–30.
6   Ibid., p. 37.
7   Kölsch 2019, p. 31.
8   See O'Callaghan 2008.
9   Philipsz quoted in the program
    of *Mourning: On Loss and Change*.
10  See youtube.com/watch?v=D-Sunoi
    BQ1.
11  Christov-Bakargiev in Philipsz 2014,
    p. 97.
12  Ibid., p. 98.
13  From the program brochure of the
    project *375 Berceuses pour Montréal*.
14  See: bercerletemps.com.
15  Harrison 2003, p. ix.

# References

— Albright, Ann Cooper (2020).
'Being Alone Together: Alain Platel
and the "Disturbance of Violent
Relatedness."' In *The Choreopolitics
of Alain Platel's les ballets C de la B:
Emotions, Gestures, Politics*, edited by
Christel Stalpaert, Guy Cools, and
Hildegard De Vuyst, pp. 69–85.
London: Bloomsbury.
—. (2001). 'Moving Contexts.' In
*Dance: Distinct Language and
Cross-Cultural Influences*, edited by
Chantal Pontbriand, pp. 41–51.
Parachute: Montréal.
—. (1997). *Choreographing Difference:
The Body and Identity in Contemporary
Dance*. Middletown: Wesleyan
University Press.
— Alexiou, Margaret (1974, 2002).
*The Ritual Lament in Greek Tradition*,
2nd ed. Maryland: Rowman &
Littlefield.
— Altena, Herman (1994). *De Perzen:
Aeschylus*. Baarn: Ambo.
— Ashenburg, Katherine (2002).
*The Mourner's Dance: What We Do
When People Die*. New York: North
Point Press.
— Assmann, Jan (2000). 'Re-membering
Osiris: From the Death Cult to
Cultural Memory.' In *ReMembering
the Body*, edited by Gabrielle
Brandstetter and Hortensia Volkers,
pp. 44–78. Ostfildern-Ruit: Hatje
Cantz Publishers.
— Barnes, Julian (2013). *Levels of Life*.
London: Jonathan Cape.
—. (2011). *The Sense of an Ending*.
London: Jonathan Cape.
— Barthes, Roland (2009). *Journal
de deuil*. Paris: Éditions du Seuil.
— Bays, Jan Chozen (2002).
*Jizo Bodhisattva: Guardian of Children,
Travelers and Other Voyagers*.
Boston: Shambhala Publications.
— Brecht, Bertolt (1950). *The Street
Scene: A Basic Model for an Epic
Theatre*, translated by John Willet,
from *Versuche 10*. head.hesge.ch/
arts-action/IMG/pdf/The_Street_
Scene_A_Basic_Model_for_an_
Epic_Theatre.pdf.
— Brizzell, Cindy, and André Lepecki,
eds. (2003). 'On Dramaturgy:
The Labor of the Question.'
*Women & Performance: A Journal of
Feminist Theory* 13, no. 2,
Issue 26.
— Buckley, Cara (2019). 'Apocalyps Got
You Down? Maybe This Will Help,'
*The New York Times*, November 17.

— Buckmaster, Sue (1997).
'A Psychoanalytical Study of the
Power of the Puppet' (unpublished
MA thesis). University of Essex.
— Butler, Judith (2020). *The Force of
Nonviolence*. London: Verso.
—. (2004). *Precarious Life: The Powers
of Mourning and Violence*.
London: Verso.
— Charles-Dominique, Luc (2011). 'Les
poids des codes symboliques et de la
prédétermination dans l'expression
musicale de la souffrance et de la
déchirure.' *Revue Insistance:
L'inconscient et ses musiques*, no. 5,
pp. 83–95.
— Cherkaoui, Sidi Larbi, with Justin
Morin (2006). *Pèlerinage sur soi*.
Arles: Actes Sud.
— Cixous, Hélène (1998). *Stigmata*.
Abingdon: Routledge.
—. (1991). *'Coming to Writing' and
Other Essays*. Cambridge: Harvard
University Press.
— Collins, Michele (2016). *The Sounds
of Grief: The Practice and Tradition of
caoineadh*. RTE Radio Player. Lyric
Feature, February 1st, 2016.
soundcloud.com/the-lyric-feature/
the-sounds-of-grief.
—. (2014). 'Caoine: Spaces for
Vocalising Grief: The De-ritualisation
and Re-ritualisation of Keening in
Contemporary Ireland' (MA thesis).
Telemark University College.
openarchive.usn.no/usn-xmlui/
handle/11250/2439081.
— Cools, Guy (2017). 'Dance
Dramaturgy as a Creative and
Somatic Practice/The Art of
Witnessing.' In *Re:Search—Dance
Dramaturgy*, edited by Carlotta
Scioldo, pp. 112–135. Turin:
Workspace Ricerca X.
—. (2016). *Imaginative Bodies:
Dialogues in Performance Practices*.
Amsterdam: Valiz.
—. (2015). *In-Between Dance Cultures:
On the Migratory Artistic Identity of
Sidi Larbi Cherkaoui and Akram Khan*.
Amsterdam: Valiz.
—. (2011). 'Giving a Voice to
Mourning.' In *Receptions of Antiquity*,
edited by Jan Nelis, pp. 145–151.
Ghent: Academia Press.
— Corradi Fiumara, Gemma (1990).
*The Other Side of Language: A
Philosophy of Listening*. Oxon:
Routledge.
— Critchley, Simon (2019). *Tragedy: The
Greeks, and Us*. London: Profile Books.

— Čufer, Eda (1997). 'Over een boom, een varken en steenkool.' *Etcetera* XV, 61, pp. 42–45.

— Daddario, Will, and Joanna Zerdy. *To Grieve, Podcast.* www.willdaddario.com/to-grieve-podcast.html.

—. (2015). 'To Grieve.' *Performance Philosophy* 1, no. 1, pp. 265–281. performancephilosophy.org/journal/article/view/10/27.

— Dakovanou, Xanthoula (2012, 2013). 'Quand l'âme chante: La voix mélodique et son pouvoir affectif.' *L' Esprit du temps* 120, pp. 21–37.

— Danforth, Loring (1982). *The Death Rituals of Rural Greece.* Princeton: Princeton University Press.

— Delecroix, Vincent, and Philippe Forest (2015). *Le deuil: Entre le chagrin et le néant.* Paris: Philo éditions.

— Despret, Vinciane (2015, 2017). *Au bonheur des morts: Récits de ceux qui restent.* Paris: Éditions La Découverte.

— Dillard, Anne (2017). *Teaching a Stone to Talk.* Edinburgh: Canongate.

— Duggan, Patrick (2012). *Trauma-Tragedy: Symptoms of Contemporary Performance.* Manchester: Manchester University Press.

— Etchells, Tim (1999). *Certain Fragments: Contemporary Performance and Forced Entertainment.* London: Routledge.

— Fabião, Eleonora (2003). 'Dramaturging with Mabou Mines: Six Proposals for *Ecco Porco*.' In *On Dramaturgy: The Labor of the Question*, Issue 26 of *Women & Performance: A Journal of Feminist Theory* 13, no. 2, pp. 29–40.

— Fisher, Mark (2014). *Ghosts of My Life: Writings on Depression, Hauntology and Lost Futures.* London: Zero Books.

— Forest, Philippe (2007). *Tous les enfants sauf un: Essai.* Paris: Gallimard.

—. (2004). *Sarinagara.* Paris: Gallimard.

—. (1997). *L'enfant éternel.* Paris: Gallimard.

— Gross, Kenneth (2011). *Puppet: An Essay on Uncanny Life.* Chicago: University of Chicago Press.

— Hallam, Elizabeth, and Jenny Hocky (2001). *Death, Memory and Material Culture.* Oxford: Berg.

— Haraway, Donna J. (2016). *Staying with the Trouble: Making Kin in the Chtulucene.* Durham: Duke University Press.

— Harrison, Robert Pogue (2003). *The Dominion of the Dead.* Chicago: University of Chicago Press.

— HAU (2017). *Unacknowledged Loss: Kunst und Rituale.* Berlin: Theater der Zeit.

— Heaney, Seamus (1966). *Death of a Naturalist.* London: Faber and Faber.

— Holst-Warhaft, Gail (1992, 1995). *Dangerous Voices: Women's Laments in Greek Literature.* London: Routledge.

— Kang, Han (2017). *The White Book*, translated by Deborah Smith. London: Portobello Books.

— Kanter, Jodi (2007). *Performing Loss: Rebuilding Community through Theater and Writing.* Southern Illinois: Southern Illinois University Press.

— Keleman, Stanley (1999). *Myth & the Body: A Colloquy with Joseph Campbell.* Berkeley: Center Press.

— Kentridge, William (2015). *More Sweetly Play the Dance.* Amsterdam: Eye Filmmuseum.

— Kessler, David (2019). *Finding Meaning: The Sixth Stage of Grief.* London: Penguin Random House.

— King, Christopher C. (2018). *Lament from Epirus: An Odyssey into Europe's Oldest Surviving Folk Music.* New York: W.W. Norton.

— Kitamura, Katie (2017). *A Separation.* London: Profile Books.

— Kölle, Brigitte (2020). 'Trauern: Von Verlust und Veränderung/Mourning: On Loss and Change.' In exhib. cat. *Trauern: Von Verlust und Veränderung/Mourning: On Loss and Change*, edited by Birgitte Kölle, Jan Steinke, and Inga Dreesen, [pp. 3–4]. Hamburg (Hamburger Kunsthalle).

— Kölsch, Stefan (2019). *Good Vibrations: Die Heilende Kraft der Musik.* Berlin: Ullstein Verlag.

— Kübler-Ross, Elisabeth, and David Kessler (2005). *On Grief and Grieving: Finding the Meaning of Grief Through the Five Stages of Loss.* New York: Scribner.

— Leader, Darian (2008). *The New Black: Mourning, Melancholia and Depression.* London: Penguin.

— Lehmann, Hans-Thies (2015). *Tragödie und Dramatisches Theater.* Berlin: Alexander Verlag.

—, and Primavesi, Patrick (2009). 'Dramaturgy on Shifting Grounds.' In *On Dramaturgy. Performance Research* 14, no. 3, edited by Karoline Gritzner, Patrick Primavesi, and Heike Roms, pp. 3–6. London: Routledge.

References

— Levine, Peter A. (2010). *In an Unspoken Voice: How the Body Releases Trauma and Restores Goodness*. Berkeley: North Atlantic Books.
— Lewis, C.S. (1961, 2015). *A Grief Observed: Reader's Edition*. London: Faber and Faber.
— Linkyekula, Faustin (2017). 'An Artist/Activist Moving (Across) Borders.' In *Moving (Across) Borders: Performing Translation, Intervention, Participation*, edited by Gabriele Brandstetter and Holger Hartung, pp. 135–155. Bielefeld: transcript Verlag.
— Lispector, Clarice (1977, 1986). *The Hour of the Star*, translated by Giovanni Ponteiro. Manchester: Carcanet Press.
— McGuire, Meredith B. (2008). *Lived Religion: Faith and Practice in Everyday Life*. Oxford: Oxford University Press.
— Martel, Yann (2016). *The High Mountains of Portugal*. Edinburgh: Canongate.
—. (2001). *Life of Pi*. Toronto: Vintage Canada.
—. (1996). *Self*. Toronto: Vintage Canada.
—. (1993, 2004). *The Facts Behind the Helsinki Roccamatios and Other Stories*. Edinburgh: Canongate.
— Milstein, Cindy, ed. (2017). *Rebellious Mourning: The Collective Work of Grief*. Edinburgh: AK Press.
— Mitchell, Stephen, ed. (1982–1989). *The Selected Poetry of Rainer Maria Rilke*, translated by Stephen Mitchell. New York: Vintage International.
— Naïr, Karthika (2008). 'Gezocht: zelf.' *Toneelgeruis* no. 3, June, pp. 106–117.
— O'Callaghan, Clare (2008). 'Lullament: Lullaby and Lament Therapeutic Qualities Actualized Through Music Therapy.' *American Journal of Hospice and Palliative Medicine* 25, no. 2, pp. 93–99.
— Phelan, Peggy (1997). *Mourning Sex: Performing Public Memories*. New York: Routledge.
— Philipsz, Susan (2010). *You Are Not Alone*. Cologne: Walther König Verlag.
— Platel, Alain (2019). *Requiem pour L.* Berchem: Epo.
— Porter, Max (2015). *Grief Is the Thing with Feathers*. London: Faber and Faber.
— Raes, Barbara (2017). *Cafuné* (Karakters). Ghent: Academia Press.
— Rahimi, Atiq (2008). *Syngué Sabour: Pierre de patience*. Paris: P.O.L.
— Reitman, Nimrod (2014).

'Downscaling Lamentation: On Trope and Fratricide.' In *Encounters in Performance Philosophy*, edited by Laura Cull and Alice Lagaay, pp. 238–258. London: Palgrave Macmillan.
— Samuel, Julia (2017). *Grief Works: Stories of Life, Death and Surviving*. London: Penguin Random House.
— Sands, Kathleen M. (2008). 'Tragedy, Theology, and Feminism in the Time After Time.' In *Rethinking Tragedy*, edited by Rita Felski, pp. 82–103. Baltimore: John Hopkins University Press.
— Savage, Judith A. (1989, 2018). *Mourning Unlived Lives: A Psychological Study of Childbearing Loss*. Asheville: Chiron Publications.
— Schneider, Michael S. (1994). *A Beginner's Guide to Constructing the Universe: The Mathematical Archetypes of Nature, Art and Science*. New York: Harper Collins.
— Seremetakis, C. Nadia (1991). *The Last Word: Women, Death and Divination in Inner Mani*. Chicago: University of Chicago Press.
— Shainberg, Catherine (2005). *Kabbalah and the Power of Dreaming: Awakening the Visionary Life*. Rochester: Inner Traditions.
— Simon, Taryn (2018). *An Occupation of Loss*. London: Artangel.
—. (2017). *An Occupation of Loss*. Berlin: Hatje Cantz Verlag.
— Snelling, Lin (2015). 'Anendingbeginning.' Unpublished.
— Solnit, Rebecca (2018). *Call Them by Their True Names: American Crises (and Essays)*. Chicago: Haymarket Books.
— Sontag, Susan (2017). *Collected Stories*, edited by Benjamin Taylor. New York: Penguin Random House.
— Stalpaert, Christel (2020). 'Troubled Pasts and Presents, Differential Futures.' In *The Choreopolitics of Alain Platel's les ballets C de la B: Emotions, Gestures, Politics*, edited by Christel Stalpaert, Guy Cools, and Hildegard De Vuyst, pp. 230–250. London: Bloomsbury.
—. (2009). 'A Dramaturgy of the Body.' In *Performance Research: On Dramaturgy* 14, no. 3, pp. 121–125. Edited by Karoline Gritzner, Patrick Primavesi, and Heike Roms. Abingdon: Routledge.
— Thielemans, Johan (1995). 'Troje, of er valt niets meer te klagen.' *Etcetera*, 13,

no. 50, pp. 42–48.

— Thiersch, Stephanie, ed. (2020). *Bilderschlachten: Bataille d'Images: A Choreographic and Musical Fresco in Words and Pictures*. Cologne: Mouvoir.

— Thorsnes, Per Roar (2015). *Docudancing Griefscapes: Choreographic Strategies for Embodying Traumatic Contexts in the Trilogy Life & Death* (Acta Scenica; 44). Helsinki: University of the Arts.

— Turkle, Sherry (2011). *Alone Together: Why We Expect More from Technology and Less From Each Other*. New York: Hachette Book Group.

— Van Dooren, Thom (2014). *Flight Ways: Life and Loss at the Edge of Extinction*. New York: Columbia University Press.

— Varvantakis, Christos (2013). 'Emotion, Performance & Death Ritual in Inner Mani' (unpublished PhD). Berlin: Freie Universität.

— Vincent-Buffault, Anne (1986). *Histoire des larmes: XVIIIe-XIXe siècles*. Paris: Editions Rivages.

— Vuong, Ocean (2019). *On Earth We're Briefly Gorgeous*. London: Jonathan Cape.

— Wickett, Elizabeth (2010). *For the Living and the Dead: The Funerary Laments of Upper Egypt, Ancient and Modern*. London: Tauris.

— Wilce, James M. (2009). *Crying Shame: Metaculture, Modernity and the Exaggerated Death of Lament*. Oxford: Wiley-Blackwell.

— Wu, Hung (2009). *Waste Not: Zhao Xiangyuan and Song Dong*. Tokyo: Tokyo Gallery and BTAP.

References

# Index

# Acknowledgments

This book has been a lifelong journey, on which I have been accompanied by many people. It would be impossible to list all of them.

First and foremost, I would like to thank Xanthoula Dakouvano, Lia Haraki, Georgina Kakoudaki, Sofia Michopoulou, Eleni Varopoulou and Katerina Zakka—all of them, in their unique ways, powerful Greek or Cypriot women—for introducing me to Greek culture and guiding me on my journey in it.

I am also very grateful to all the artists I have dialogued with in this book. I had the pleasure of collaborating with many of them, accompanying their creative processes, sharing their insecurities and doubts, but also their discoveries and joys.

At different stages of the writing process, several institutions supported this book by giving me the necessary time to focus on its topic. But as always, it is not the institution itself, but the people working there who make the biggest difference: Holger Hartung and Christel Weiler at the International Research Center 'Interweaving Performance Cultures' of the Freie Universität in Berlin; Yana Meerzon, Daniel Mroz, and Sylvain Shryburt at the theater department of the University of Ottawa; and Piet Defraye and Lin Snelling at the theater department of the University of Alberta. I received ongoing support from Christel Stalpaert at the University of Ghent, whose research center S.P.A.M. has generously offered me an academic home over the years, even if I have seldom been physically present there.

Other colleagues and friends have generously sponsored the production of this book through their companies or artistic structures. They are: Jean Abreu Dance, les ballets C de la B (Alain Platel and Lieven Thyrion), Eastman (Sidi Larbi Cherkaoui), Cie Mouvoir (Stephanie Thiersch), Muzeum Susch (Joanna Leśneriowska), Stichting SHARP (Arno Schuitemaker and Joriene Blom) and Siamese Cie (Koen Augustijnen and Rosalba Torres Guerrero).

The practical realization of this book would not have been possible without Lisa Marie Bowler, my copy editor, who, as with my previous books, upgrades my English without changing my personal style; and Pia Pol and Astrid Vorstermans at my publisher Valiz, who have guided the manuscript through all the stages of the production process with a care that is exceptional in the international publishing business.

To all of the above, I am very grateful for their ongoing support.

Finally, this book would not exist without my family: my mother Charlotte, my brother Luc and his family, my three sons Filip, Steven, and Julian and their mothers Diane and Stephanie. They all had to live with 'my mourning' at different stages and in different intensities, but they were always there for me. Perhaps without realizing it, their presence in my life and their unconditional love kept my interests and desires firmly rooted on this side of the 'threshold' of life. If, as many have acknowledged, mourning is the flipside of love, then this equation can also be reversed: in the end, love is the best therapy for grief. The laments are just one powerful expression of this love.

Vienna, 2021

# About the Author

**Guy Cools** is a Belgian dance dramaturg, currently living in Vienna. He has worked as a dance critic and dance curator. From 1990 till 2002, he curated the dance program of Arts Centre Vooruit in Ghent, Belgium. As a production dramaturg, he worked with artists such as Jean Abreu (UK), Koen Augustijnen (BE), Sidi Larbi Cherkaoui (BE), Danièle Desnoyers (CA), Alexander Gottfarb (AT), Lia Haraki (CY), Akram Khan (UK), Joshua Monten (SUI), Arno Schuitemaker (NL) and Stephanie Thiersch (DE). With the Canadian choreographer Lin Snelling, he developed an improvised performance practice Rewriting Distance, which focuses on the integration of movement, voice, and writing.

As a dramaturgical mentor, he has coached Anghiari Dance Hub, the International Choreographer's Week in Tilburg, the project Danse et Dramaturgie in Switzerland, the Biennale Dance College in Venice and the Atlas program of Impulstanz in Vienna. He is a Postdoctoral Researcher at Ghent University, where he completed a practice-based PhD on the relationship between dance and writing. He lectures and teaches at various universities and arts colleges in Europe and Canada, including the University of Ottawa and the Fontys School of Fine and Performing Arts in Tilburg.

His most recent publications include *The Ethics of Art: Ecological Turns in the Performing Arts*, co-edited with Pascal Gielen (Valiz, 2014); *In-between Dance Cultures: On the Migratory Artistic Identity of Sidi Larbi Cherkaoui and Akram Khan* (Valiz, 2015); *Imaginative Bodies: Dialogues in Performance Practices* (Valiz, 2016) and *The Choreopolitics of Alain Platel's les ballets C de la B*, co-edited with Christel Stalpaert and Hildegard De Vuyst (Bloomsbury, 2019).

# Partners

**Eastman/Sidi Larbi Cherkaoui**

Founded in January 2010, Eastman was set up to produce and promote the work of its artistic director Sidi Larbi Cherkaoui. Cherkaoui's non-hierarchical thinking on movement, body language, and culture is the basis of his artistic approach. His works offer the audience a vast array of projects and collaborations across many art forms, including contemporary dance, theater, ballet, opera, circus, music, and film.

The slew of awards Cherkaoui has picked up across this millennium reflects this genre-transcending prolificity. They include two Olivier Awards, three Tanz awards for best choreographer (2008, 2011, 2017) and a Fred & Adele Astaire Award for Outstanding Choreography in a Feature Film. In 2018, he received the Europe Prize Theatrical Realities for 'his never-ending commitment in new collaborations with artists from all over the world' and was conferred the title of 'Commandeur dans l'ordre des Arts et des Lettres' by the French Government in 2019.

Set in his native harbor city of Antwerp and resident at deSingel International Art Campus, Eastman forms the central nexus for all of Cherkaoui's work. Since its foundation in 2010, Cherkaoui created amongst others *Babel*$^{(words)}$, *Play*, *TeZukA*, *Puz/zle*, *4D*, *Fractus V*, *Session* and *3S* under Eastman's wings. It also coordinates Cherkaoui's work for other organizations.

Eastman's international partners include La Monnaie/De Munt (Brussels), Les Théâtres de la Ville de Luxembourg, Grande Halle de la Villette (Paris), deSingel International Arts Campus (Antwerp) and Sadler's Wells (London).

Eastman is supported by the Flemish Government and the BNP Paribas Foundation and was European Cultural Ambassador 2013.

Cools worked as a dramaturg with Cherkaoui on iconic works such as *zero degrees*, *Myth* and *Aprocrifu* and continues to support the development of a discourse around his work, amongst others in *In-Between Dance Cultures: On the Migratory Artistic Identity of Sidi Larbi Cherkaoui and Akram Khan* (Valiz, 2016).

www.east-man.be

**Jean Abreu Dance**

Jean Abreu Dance was founded in 2009 as the creative engine of its artistic director, Jean Abreu.

Born in Brazil, Jean Abreu moved to London in 1996 after receiving a scholarship to study at Trinity Laban Conservatoire for Music and Dance. In 2003 he was awarded the Jerwood Choreography Award and became an Associate Artist at The Place in London. Jean has been a movement director for fashion magazines and global advertising campaigns and also a regular visiting dance artist/lecturer at renowned dance institutions worldwide.

Our work researches and uses the body as a tool to articulate human emotions, memories, sensations, and desires. We believe the body holds the key to explain who we are and how we feel, giving us a primal and universal language to communicate with and connect to others. Dance demands us to accept and to surrender to uncertainty and impermanence. Its true meaning exists in the shared experience between the performing body and the spectator's. Collaboration is another fundamental aspect of our creative process and often our productions dialogue with artists from other disciplines. We use movement and choreography, contemporary music, visual arts, design, and digital technology to create dance performances that celebrate the transformative nature of human identity.

Jean Abreu Dance presents work locally, internationally, and via online spaces, reaching audiences across the globe. Committed to broadening access to dance, Jean Abreu Dance's creative learning program provides inspiring opportunities for community groups, young people and professionals.

Jean Abreu met dance dramaturg Guy Cools in 2004 and since 2016 they have been collaborating on numerous projects including: *A Thread* (2016), *Solo for Two* (2018) and more recently *As They Are*, *Mantras for the body* (working title), a work exploring laments, grief, and the power of vulnerability.

Jean Abreu Dance is supported by Arts Council England | Lottery Fund

www.jeanabreudance.com

**les ballets C de la B/Alain Platel**

In 1984, les ballets C de la B (Ghent, Belgium) was founded by Alain Platel, together with some friends and members of his family. Since then, it has become a company that enjoys great success at home and abroad. Over the years it has developed into an artistic platform for a variety of choreographers and dancers. The company still keeps to its principle of enabling artists from various disciplines and backgrounds to take part in the dynamic creative process.

The company seeks to share the knowhow, the artistic capital, and the network that is built up with every production. les ballets C de la B attaches great importance to pass on and explore a vast variety of (dancing) techniques and is constantly looking for ways to connect with others. Since 2010, organizing workshops has been one of the activities of les ballets C de la B.

From 2017 onward, les ballets C de la B has been investing—besides in production—in development by launching a residency program. These projects are labelled in Co-laBo. The projects selected for the residency program have an ambitious intention and need the temporary collaboration as a necessary stage in the creation process of the project.

As a result of its 'unique mixture of artistic visions,' les ballets C de la B is not easy to classify. It is nevertheless possible to discern something like a house style (popular, anarchic, eclectic, committed), and its motto is 'this dance is for the world and the world is for everyone.'

When Cools was the dance curator of the arts Centre Vooruit in Ghent, from 1990 till 2002, he invited les ballets C de la B as house company. Over the years he had held many public talks with Alain Platel and he is one of the co-editors of *The Choreopolitics of Alain Platel's les ballets C de la B* (Bloomsbury, 2019).

www.lesballetscdela.be

**MOUVOIR Company/Stephanie Thiersch**

MOUVOIR Company is the structure that supports the work of the German choreographer Stephanie Thiersch. With MOUVOIR she develops stage performances, films, and installations. MOUVOIR deals with the central topics of our modern lives, in a manner that is both authentic and experimental.

Thiersch considers her choreographic work as being part of a broader paradigm of interdisciplinary movement research, which initially involved media, then increasingly visual arts, and more recently integrates music in the choreographic mindset. As an uncompromising observer Stephanie Thiersch dissects her environment. She is interested in physical and emotional states that defy a clear definition and oscillate between their own various media representations. Thiersch's interest is directed at the body in the process of transformation and transition debating community-forming processes. Around the artistic work MOUVOIR developed a fringe program labelled *Be our guest*, in which the notion of 'hospitality' that resonates in the artistic work is translated into practical and theoretical formats for audience and professionals alike.

Since 2011 Thiersch has also been creating collective work, addressing the subject of postcolonialism with artists from sub-Saharan Africa. In 2016, she organized *City Dance Köln*, based on an idea from and in cooperation with dance pioneer Anna Halprin. The politically motivated manifestation involved 600 performers and over 10,000 participating passers-by moving and dancing through the city of Cologne. In 2021, she will premiere *Archipel*, with dancers, musicians, and a choir performing in an architectural landscape by Sou Fujimoto.

Together with Greek musician and composer Martha Mavroidi, Thiersch has embarked on researching the *moirológhia* and how the narratives of these laments can show us ways into the future. The result, *Hello Emptiness—Songs for Future Laments*, will bring together dancers, a countertenor, and a choir.

Cools has worked with Thiersch as a dramaturg on the stage performance *Bronze by Gold* and on the installation piece *The Memory Machine*.

www.mouvoir.de

**Muzeum Susch**

Muzeum Susch is located in the valley of the river Inn (CH), amongst the remnants of a medieval monastery set against the backdrop of alpine mountains. To host the museum, the existing structures were subtly restored and recombined in an inspiring environment for artistic contemplation and mediation, introducing spaces for exhibitions as well as for experimental presentations, conference lectures, and events as well as an interdisciplinary residency program.

Founded and opened in January 2019 by Grażyna Kulczyk, Polish entrepreneur and long-term supporter of contemporary art, Muzeum Susch is specifically (but not exclusively) informed by her deep interest in and understanding of women artists. Its program seeks an emotional connection to art as a matrilineage of the sometimes omitted, overlooked, or misread and its collection is focused on and contributes to the recognition and greater visibility of conceptual art and female artists with a natural input of Central Eastern European art. One of the central qualities of Muzeum Susch and its activities is the redefinition of the canonical and the marginalized, not as a dominating force that silences others, but as an influential voice for making other voices heard.

Being simultaneously a site of contemplation, research and artistic intervention, Muzeum Susch has knowledge production and reflection in its DNA and aims to become a place where exhibitions and other programs ask and explore new questions rather than report pre-existing knowledge. With its program Acziun, dedicated to choreographic reflection, as well as with its interdisciplinary residency program Temporars and the research-based Instituto Susch, Muzeum Susch constitutes the first institutional hub of contemporary art in the Engadin Valley. The annual magazine *Susch* serves as an additional thought-provoking platform.

Muzeum Susch/Acziun Susch supported publishing of this book. It offered Cools a residence to continue his research on laments in contemporary art and commissioned a podcast on the subject for their 2020 series *Echolot*.

www.muzeumsusch.ch

**SHARP/ArnoSchuitemaker**

Reapproaching performance art and dance, Arno Schuitemaker creates works one has to experience. Through a strong integration of ongoing, evolving movement with electronic music and impressive lighting designs, his interdisciplinary performances immerse the audience, each in their unique way. They stretch and alter the way we perceive time and space and transform into embodied meditations on life, reflecting the depths of our existence. Rooted in the pages of his diary, Schuitemaker's artistic research progresses consciously and continuously from project to project. Each work builds on the previous and leads to the next.

In October 2019, *The Way You Sound Tonight*, Schuitemaker's most recent work, which premiered at the Holland Festival in Amsterdam, was honored as the most impressive dance production by the VSCD—the Oscar of Dutch dance. *The Way You Sound Tonight* is presented in (potentially infinite) cycles for different audience groups and forms a multi-layered universe that incorporates the inevitable passing of time.

Cools has been accompanying Schuitemaker's artistic development since 2010 and has been the production dramaturg of his work since 2014, including *I is an Other*, *WHILE WE STRIVE*, *I will wait for you*, *If You Could See Me Now* and the acclaimed *The Way You Sound Tonight*.

Schuitemaker's work has been presented at renowned venues and contemporary performing arts festivals in over twenty countries. His company, SHARP/ArnoSchuitemaker, is based in Amsterdam, the Netherlands.

www.arnoschuitemaker.com

**Siamese Cie/Koen Augustijnen and Rosalba Torres Guerrero**
Siamese Cie is the artistic name of Koen Augustijnen and Rosalba
Torres Guerrero. For more than twenty years, Koen Augustijnen
and Rosalba Torres Guerrero have been part of the Belgian and
international dance landscape. Koen Augustijnen worked with Alain
Platel's les ballets C de la B, initially as a dancer. From 1997 until
2013 he was one of the company's house choreographers. From 1997
until 2005, Rosalba Torres Guerrero was one of the core members
of Anne Teresa De Keersmaeker's Rosas. After that she joined
les ballets C de la B for ten years. In 2013 Augustijnen and Torres
Guerreo co-created, together with Hildegard De Vuyst *Badke*,
a piece for ten Palestinian dancers produced by KVS, les ballets C
de la B, and The Qattan foundation. Based on this shared artistic
history, they created Siamese Cie to support each other's work and
develop new projects together, such as *(B)* (2019), a choreography
with professional boxers and contemporary dancers.

Siamese means 'conjoined, unified, fused together.'
Augustijnen and Torres Guerrero make independent productions
that are intended to celebrate diversity and plurality and have a
preference for cross-overs between different genres, cultures,
languages, and traditions. The duo's choice for 'dance theater' is
motivated by the belief in the vitality of dance and the expressive
possibilities of its rough and physical energy. They aim at translat-
ing emotional states into physical performance and dance.

In the past, Cools has worked with Augustijnen on productions such as *bâche* (2004), *IMPORT/EXPORT* (2006), and *Ashes*
(2009). He is also the dramaturgical adviser, together with the
Greek dramaturg Georgina Kakoudaki, for the most recent productions of Siamese Cie, *Lamenta* (2021), which is entirely based
on the Greek tradition of the *moirológhia*.

The two choreographers of Siamese Cie are associated
artists with La Comédie de Clermont-Ferrand—scène nationale.

www.siamese-cie.be

# Antennae-
# Arts in Society
# Book Series

**Antennae-Arts in Society Series**

Antennae-Arts in Society is a peer-reviewed book series that validates artistic, critical, speculative and essayistic writing as a full academic publishing method. Contributions to the series look upon the arts as 'antennae', feelers for the cultural interpretation and articulation of topical political, economic, social, technological or environmental issues.

The books in this series bring together audiences of diverse backgrounds: artists and other creative makers, academics and researchers from various disciplines, critics, writers, journalists, politicians, curators, and institutional parties, who wish to broaden their view in different political, social and other contexts.

Proposals for book concepts in all artistic and scientific disciplines that take culture as the base of interpretation for the social fabric of our contemporary lives are welcomed and will be considered for publication by the academic board.

*Editorial board Valiz—Arts in Society book series*:
Pascal Gielen, Professor of Sociology of Culture & Politics, at the Antwerp Research Institute for the Arts (Antwerp University—Belgium), also leads the Culture Commons Quest Office (CCQO)
Thijs Lijster, Assistant Professor in the Philosophy of Art and Culture at the University of Groningen, and researcher at the Culture Commons Quest Office of the University of Antwerp
Astrid Vorstermans, Publisher Valiz

# Colophon

## Colophon

**Performing Mourning**
*Laments in Contemporary Art*

*Author*
Guy Cools

*Editing*
Lisa Marie Bowler

Antennae-Arts in Society Series N° 30
by Valiz, Amsterdam

*Copy Editing*
Leo Reijnen

*Proofreading*
Els Brinkman

*Design*
Metahaven

*Paper Inside*
Munken Print 100 gr 1.5

*Paper Cover*
Munken Pure 240 gr

*Printing and Binding*
Wilco Art Books, Amersfoort

*Publisher*
Valiz, Amsterdam, 2021
www.valiz.nl

ISBN 978-94-92095-98-5

This publication was made possible through the generous support of

- Eastman, Antwerp (BE)
  www.east-man.be
- Jean Abreu Dance, Luton (UK)
  www.jeanabreudance.com
- les ballets C de la B, Ghent (BE)
  www.lesballetscdela.be
- Mouvoir, Cologne (DE)
  www.mouvoir.de
- Muzeum Susch (CH)/Art Stations
  Foundation, Poznan (PL)
  www.muzeumsusch.ch,
  www.artstationsfoundation5050.com
- Siamese Cie., Brussels (BE)
  www.siamese-cie.be
- SHARP, Amsterdam (NL)
  www.arnoschuitemaker.com

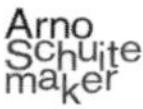


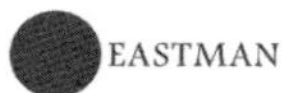


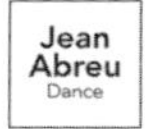




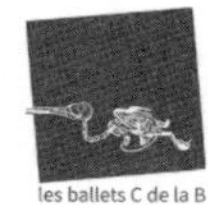


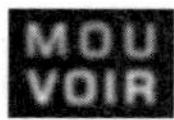

*Distribution*
USA/Canada/Latin America: D.A.P.,
www.artbook.com
GB/IE: Anagram Books,
www.anagrambooks.com
NL/BE/LU: Centraal Boekhuis,
www.cb.nl
Europe/Asia: Idea Books,
www.ideabooks.nl
Australia: Perimeter Books,
www.perimeterdistribution.com

ISBN 978-94-92095-98-5

Printed and bound in the Netherlands

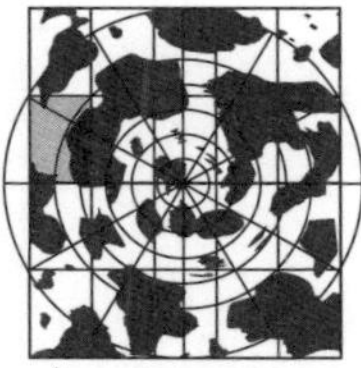

**Antennae**

# Antennae Series

Antennae N° 1
**The Fall of the Studio**
*Artists at Work*
edited by Wouter Davidts & Kim Paice
Amsterdam: Valiz, 2009
(2nd ed.: 2010),
ISBN 978-90-78088-29-5

Antennae N° 2
**Take Place**
*Photography and Place
from Multiple Perspectives*
edited by Helen Westgeest
Amsterdam: Valiz, 2009,
ISBN 978-90-78088-35-6

Antennae N° 3
**The Murmuring of the
Artistic Multitude**
*Global Art, Memory and Post-Fordism*
Pascal Gielen (author)
Arts *in* Society
Amsterdam: Valiz, 2009
(2nd ed.: 2011),
ISBN 978-90-78088-34-9

Antennae N° 4
**Locating the Producers**
*Durational Approaches to Public Art*
edited by Paul O'Neill & Claire
Doherty
Amsterdam: Valiz, 2011,
ISBN 978-90-78088-51-6

Antennae N° 5
**Community Art**
*The Politics of Trespassing*
edited by Paul De Bruyne &
Pascal Gielen
Arts *in* Society
Amsterdam: Valiz, 2011 (2nd ed.: 2013),
ISBN 978-90-78088-50-9

Antennae N° 6
**See it Again, Say it Again**
*The Artist as Researcher*
edited by Janneke Wesseling
Amsterdam: Valiz, 2011,
ISBN 978-90-78088-53-0

Antennae N° 7
**Teaching Art in the
Neoliberal Realm**
*Realism versus Cynicism*
edited by Pascal Gielen &
Paul De Bruyne
Arts *in* Society
Amsterdam: Valiz, 2012
(2nd ed.: 2013),
ISBN 978-90-78088-57-8

Antennae N° 8
**Institutional Attitudes**
*Instituting Art in a Flat World*
edited by Pascal Gielen
Arts *in* Society
Amsterdam: Valiz, 2013,
ISBN 978-90-78088-68-4

Antennae N° 9
**Dread**
*The Dizziness of Freedom*
edited by Juha van 't Zelfde
Amsterdam: Valiz, 2013,
ISBN 978-90-78088-81-3

Antennae N° 10
**Participation Is Risky**
*Approaches to Joint Creative Processes*
edited by Liesbeth Huybrechts
Amsterdam: Valiz, 2014,
ISBN 978-90-78088-77-6

Antennae N° 11
**The Ethics of Art**
*Ecological Turns in the Performing Arts*
edited by Guy Cools & Pascal Gielen
Arts *in* Society
Amsterdam: Valiz, 2014,
ISBN 978-90-78088-87-5

Antennae N° 12
**Alternative Mainstream**
*Making Choices in Pop Music*
Gert Keunen (author)
Arts *in* Society
Amsterdam: Valiz, 2014,
ISBN 978-90-78088-95-0

Antennae N° 13
**The Murmuring of the Artistic**
*Global Art, Politics and Post-Fordism*
Pascal Gielen (author)
Completely revised and enlarged
edition of Antennae N° 3
Arts *in* Society
Amsterdam: Valiz, 2015,
ISBN 978-94-92095-04-6

Antennae N° 14
**Aesthetic Justice**
*Intersecting Artistic and Moral Perspectives*
edited by Pascal Gielen &
Niels Van Tomme
Arts *in* Society
Amsterdam: Valiz, 2015,
ISBN 978-90-78088-86-8

Antennae N° 15
**No Culture, No Europe**
*On the Foundation of Politics*
edited by Pascal Gielen
Arts *in* Society
Amsterdam: Valiz, 2015,
ISBN 978-94-92095-03-9

Antennae N° 16
**Arts Education Beyond Art**
*Teaching Art in Times of Change*
edited by Barend van Heusden &
Pascal Gielen
Arts *in* Society
Amsterdam: Valiz, 2015,
ISBN 978-90-78088-85-1

Antennae N° 17
**Mobile Autonomy**
*Exercises in Artists' Self-Organization*
edited by Nico Dockx & Pascal
Gielen
Arts *in* Society
Amsterdam: Valiz, 2015,
ISBN 978-94-92095-10-7

Antennae N° 18
**Moving Together**
*Theorizing and Making
Contemporary Dance*
Rudi Laermans (author)
Arts *in* Society
Amsterdam: Valiz, 2015,
ISBN 978-90-78088-52-3

Antennae N° 19
**Spaces for Criticism**
*Shifts in Contemporary Art Discourses*
edited by Thijs Lijster, Suzana
Milevska, Pascal Gielen,
Ruth Sonderegger
Arts *in* Society
Amsterdam: Valiz, 2015,
ISBN 978-90-78088-75-2

Antennae N° 20
**Interrupting the City**
*Artistic Constitutions of the Public Sphere*
edited by Sander Bax, Pascal Gielen
& Bram Ieven
Arts *in* Society
Amsterdam: Valiz, 2015,
ISBN 978-94-92095-02-2

Antennae N° 21
**In-between Dance Cultures**
*On the Migratory Artistic Identity of
Sidi Larbi Cherkaoui and Akram Khan*
Guy Cools (author)
Arts *in* Society
Amsterdam: Valiz, 2015,
ISBN 978-94-92095-11-4

Antennae N° 22
**Imaginative Bodies**
*Dialogues in Performance Practices*
Guy Cools (author)
Arts *in* Society
Amsterdam: Valiz, 2016,
ISBN 978-94-92095-20-6

Antennae N° 23
**The Practice of Dramaturgy**
*Working on Actions in Performance*
edited by Konstantina Georgelou,
Efrosini Protopapa,
Danae Theodoridou
Arts *in* Society
Amsterdam: Valiz, 2017,
ISBN: 978-94-92095-18-3

Antennae N° 24
**The Art of Civil Action**
*Political Space and Cultural Dissent*
edited by Philipp Dietachmair,
Pascal Gielen
Arts *in* Society
Amsterdam: Valiz, 2017,
ISBN: 978-94-92095-39-8

Antennae N° 25
**Commonism**
*A New Aesthetics of the Real*
Nico Dockx & Pascal Gielen
Arts *in* Society
Amsterdam: Valiz, 2018,
ISBN 978-94-92095-47-3

Colophon

Antennae N° 26
**The Future of the New**
*Artistic Innovation in Times
of Social Acceleration*
Thijs Lijster (ed.)
Arts *in* Society
Amsterdam: Valiz, 2018,
ISBN 978-94-92095-58-9

Antennae N° 27
**Contemporary Artist Residencies**
*Reclaiming Time and Space*
edited by Taru Elfving, Pascal Gielen,
Irmeli Kokko
Arts *in* Society
Amsterdam: Valiz, 2019,
ISBN 978-94-92095-46-6

Antennae N° 28
**When Fact Is Fiction**
*Documentary Art in the Post-Truth Era*
edited by Nele Wynants
Arts *in* Society
Amsterdam: Valiz, 2020,
ISBN 978-94-92095-71-8

Antennae N° 29
**The Aesthetics of Ambiguity**
*Understanding and Addressing
Monoculture*
Pascal Gielen & Nav Haq (eds.)
Arts *in* Society
Amsterdam: Valiz, 2020,
ISBN 978-94-92095-76-3